NEWS THAT STAYS NEWS

Simon Rae is author of the widely acclaim[ed] ... and editor of *The Faber Book of Drink, Drin*[k] ... *Faber Book of Murder* and *The Faber Book* ... years he was presenter of the BBC Radio ... *Please!,* and he has also written and prese[nted] numerous other radio programmes, including an award-winning life of John Clare. He contributed topical poems to the *Guardian* for ten years, and published two collections of them, *Soft Targets* and *Rapid Response.*

Nick,

Enjoy! Thanks for all the laughs, and for your friendship.
Merry Christmas 2001.

Laura xxx.

NEWS THAT STAYS NEWS

The Twentieth Century in Poems

edited by Simon Rae

ff

faber and faber

First published in 1999
by Faber and Faber Limited
3 Queen Square London WC1N 3AU

Photoset by Wilmaset Ltd, Wirral
Printed in England by Clays Ltd, St Ives plc

A CIP record for this book
is available from the British Library

ISBN 0-571-20060-5

10 9 8 7 6 5 4 3 2 1

for John Caperon
friend through the last quarter

CONTENTS

INTRODUCTION

The end of a century is a fitting time for poetry anthologies.
Several have already appeared and others will follow, each
designed in some way to take stock and assess achievement and,
at least implicitly, establish hierarchies of excellence. The idea
behind this book is rather different. It is, very simply, to build up
a picture of the twentieth century by selecting a poem for each
year from 1900 to 1999. Each poet is rationed to one appearance,
and although eligibility is not dependent on nationality, the scope
has been limited to what might loosely be termed the British
experience.

In a period of rapid change, the sense of 'Britishness' itself has
undergone radical readjustments. The unquestioned certainties of
the pre-Great War period have evaporated in the face of an
inevitable (and now largely unmourned) descent from imperial
and economic pre-eminence (compare and contrast John
Davidson's 'Song for the Twenty-fourth of May', 1909, and Glyn
Maxwell's 'Video Tale of a Patriot', 1992). While Britain's standing
in the world has declined, the position of just over half the
population – viz., women – has improved. The hopes implicit in
Frances Cornford's 'Autumn Morning at Cambridge', 1902, would
seem to have been substantially fulfilled in U. A. Fanthorpe's
'Mother Scrubbing the Floor', 1998 (though today's eco-warriors,
veterans of Greenham Common and other dissidents would
probably find the indignities inflicted on suffragettes in Holloway
– Kathleen Emerson, 1912 – more familiar than the rest of us
would imagine). Poets have also charted the course of relations
between men and women throughout the century, and, *pace*
Philip Larkin, sex did not begin in 1963.

But for all the vast upheavals some continuities can be
discerned. Britain still has a monarchy and the recent death of a
royal figure (even one fallen from grace) provoked a tide of
national mourning echoing that for Queen Victoria ninety-six
years earlier. The short poems George Meredith and Andrew
Motion wrote on the two different occasions offer a telescoped
study in the changing parameters of reverence. And beyond the
level of the individual, however sanctified by position or the

media, those in actual charge continue, in Auden's words, 'making / the usual squalid mess called History'. The century opened with Britain embroiled in the Boer War, and at the time of writing it is apparently poised to commit ground forces in the Balkans.

This, however, is not an attempt at a chronology of the century (along the lines, say, of Kenneth Baker's *The Faber Book of English History in Verse*). Some events, most obviously the two World Wars, naturally dominate their period. Others got in – or not – as poets wrote about them, and as my eye lit on what they had written. The General Strike of 1926 (or rather, the Welsh miners' strike which sparked it off), has a poem; the hunger marches of the 1930s do not.

In pursuit of a sense of the tone and mood of the changing times, I have, by and large, insisted on contemporaneity. This precluded choosing Philip Larkin's 'MCMXIV' for 1914, for instance, or resorting to Craig Raine's *History: The Home Movie* to fill an inconvenient void in the 1920s. On the other hand, strict observance of this rule would necessarily have excluded the whole of childhood and adolescence, clearly an unacceptable sacrifice – hence the inclusion of David Scott's 'Winston Churchill' [1965] and Zulfikar Ghose's 'The Body's Independence' [1947].

Of course ability has not been spread evenly throughout the century, and the strict formula of only one poem per year (and per poet) has produced many of the elements of a crossword puzzle. Several poets have been pencilled in and then rubbed out more than once. The more accomplished a poet, the more he or she has been shunted from one slot to another. Auden, for instance, moved up and down from 1928 to 1937, and was even, briefly, a candidate for 1969.

Even with such accommodating talents to call on, there has had to be some leeway with dates, and I have permitted myself four options: date of composition, date of first publication, date of book publication, and (more rarely) the date of the event described. Appropriately enough, Empson's 'Missing Dates' provides a typical example. Clearly a Thirties poem, it was not collected until 1940 but it seemed sensible to choose it for 1937, when it was written. Similarly, Henry Reed's 'Naming of Parts', from his sequence *Lessons of the War*, did not appear between hard covers until 1946, but, on the authority of *The Voice of War*, edited by Victor Selwyn of the Salamandar Oasis Trust, I have placed it earlier, where it obviously belongs.

Even with this degree of flexibility, some years created major headaches. 1945 saw the end of the war both in Europe and the Far East, where the fighting was brought to an unexpectedly rapid halt by the detonation of atomic bombs above Hiroshima and Nagasaki. The implications of this shattering new weapon of annihilation were immediately clear, and among the poets Edith Sitwell responded with alacrity (as she had to the Blitz with 'Still Falls The Rain' in 1940). But the liberation of Europe earlier in the same momentous summer had brought the Allied armies face to face with the unspeakable horrors of the Nazi concentration camps. I chose a poem by an eye-witness who was with the first British troops to stumble into the charnel house of Belsen rather than the overblown, though undoubtedly heartfelt, rhetoric of Sitwell's 'Dirge for the New Sunrise'. Another editor would have made a different choice.

On the whole I have tried to avoid the best-known and most regularly reprinted poems, but sometimes the predictable has proved the inevitable. I decided that 'Naming of Parts' was essential (along with 'Cargoes', 'Missing Dates', and Jon Silkin's 'Death of a Son'), but happily opted for Stevie Smith's 'Touch and Go' rather than the ubiquitous 'Not Waving but Drowning'. However, as pundits pick their poem of the century, I am keenly aware that 'The Waste Land' is missing from the following pages. In the end I decided that its length would unbalance the reader's progress through the book. Though less influential, 'The Hollow Men' is just as much a poem of its time, and boasts one of the most famous quotations of the period into the bargain.

The selection throughout has been fraught with invidious choices and as the end of the century neared, the process came to resemble a game of musical chairs with frenzied furniture removal spurred on by ever more staccato bursts from the gramophone. Even those who have ended up with a seat may cavil at the poem by which they are represented ('Not my best side'). My choices cannot hope to be remotely definitive, or even authoritative, and in all probability no reader will agree with more than a handful of them. Nevertheless, the book will have achieved its aim if it manages to convey, however imperfectly, something of the century's unfolding zeitgeist and to confirm Ezra Pound's dictum that 'literature is news that stays news'.

This is not a textbook and the Notes are intended merely to help place the poems in their context without critical analysis or undue exegesis. For historical details I have drawn most heavily on *The Pimlico Chronology of British History* by Alan and Veronica Palmer. The source of quotations is generally acknowledged, but I should perhaps mention two books here which helped enormously with the Great War: Lyn MacDonald's *Somme*, which yielded the poem for 1916, and Niall Ferguson's *The Pity of War* which provided a wealth of provocative insights into the conflict.

I did most of my reading in the British Library, the London Library and the Arts Council's Poetry Library in the Royal Festival Hall, and I would like to thank their respective staffs (and in particular, Mary Enright of the Poetry Library) for their help and courtesy. Several friends showed an interest in the project and made useful suggestions, and my editor, Christopher Reid, and his assistant, Jane Feaver, have both been supportive and critically alert. My thanks to them all.

Simon Rae

April 1999

NEWS THAT STAYS NEWS

The Darkling Thrush

I leant upon a coppice gate
  When Frost was spectre-gray,
And Winter's dregs made desolate
  The weakening eye of day.
The tangled bine-stems scored the sky
  Like strings of broken lyres,
And all mankind that haunted nigh
  Had sought their household fires.

The land's sharp features seemed to be
  The Century's corpse outleant,
His crypt the cloudy canopy,
  The wind his death-lament.
The ancient pulse of germ and birth
  Was shrunken hard and dry,
And every spirit upon earth
  Seemed fervourless as I.

At once a voice arose among
  The bleak twigs overhead
In a full-hearted evensong
  Of joy illimited;
An aged thrush, frail, gaunt, and small,
  In blast-beruffled plume,
Had chosen thus to fling his soul
  Upon the growing gloom.

So little cause for carolings
  Of such ecstatic sound
Was written on terrestrial things
  Afar or nigh around,

That I could think there trembled through
    His happy good-night air
Some blessed Hope, whereof he knew
    And I was unaware.

31 December 1900

At The Funeral

February 2, 1901

Her sacred body bear: the tenement
  Of that strong soul now ranked with God's Elect.
Her heart upon her people's heart she spent;
  Hence is she Royalty's lodestar to direct.

The peace is hers, of whom all lands have praised
  Majestic virtues ere her day unseen.
Aloft the name of Womanhood she raised,
  And gave new readings to the Title, Queen.

Autumn Morning at Cambridge

I ran out in the morning, when the air was clean and new
And all the grass was glittering and grey with autumn dew,
I ran out to an apple-tree and pulled an apple down,
And all the bells were ringing in the old grey town.

Down in the town off the bridges and the grass,
They are sweeping up the leaves to let the people pass,
Sweeping up the old leaves, golden-reds and browns,
Whilst the men go to lecture with the wind in their gowns.

Cargoes

Quinquereme of Nineveh from distant Ophir
Rowing home to haven in sunny Palestine,
With a cargo of ivory,
And apes and peacocks,
Sandalwood, cedarwood, and sweet white wine.

Stately Spanish galleon coming from the Isthmus,
Dipping through the Tropics by the palm-green shores,
With a cargo of diamonds,
Emeralds, amethysts,
Topazes, and cinnamon, and gold moidores.

Dirty British coaster with a salt-caked smoke stack
Butting through the Channel in the mad March days,
With a cargo of Tyne coal,
Road-rail, pig-lead,
Firewood, iron-ware, and cheap tin trays.

Frames of Mind

'I declare that the above statement contains a full, just and true account
and return of the *whole of my income from every source whatsoever* for
the year ending the 5th day of April, 1905.'

Extract from Income Tax Return form

O Mr Surveyor of Taxes,
    A terrible task you impose!
I claim some abatement: you ask for a statement
    Of details which nobody knows.
My revenue wanes and it waxes
    Along with my varying mood;
It's mainly a question, I think, of digestion,
    And largely depends upon food.
        Then how fill up the form?
            My income how foretell?
    How know what cheer the coming year
    Is bringing near, with smile or tear?
        O, will my hearth be warm,
            My table furnished well?
    Or will my fare be sordid care,
            Another weary spell?

When late at the Carlton I tarry,
    Where riches and luxury reign,
When I sup *con amore* and trail clouds of glory
    Inspired by the best of champagne,
I am then a great playwright – a Barrie –
    Three plays at a time on the boards –
The royalties pour in and put more and more in
    My purse till it's fat as a lord's.

When Economy raises her finger
    And bids me reluctantly go
To dine for a florin in haunts that are foreign
    And doubtful in dingy Soho,

Fair visions no longer will linger,
   The future begins to look black;
I see myself earning with toil and heart-burning
   The wage of a newspaper hack.

When, growing more prudent than ever,
   On messes of pottage I sup,
Or dine somewhat sparsely on cutlets of parsley,
   And drink Adam's ale from my cup;
When I struggle with frugal endeavour
   By 'diet' to keep down the bill,
When I feel filled-and-emptied, I'm very much tempted
   To send in my income as *nil.*
      Then how fill up the form?
         My income how foretell?
      How know what cheer the coming year
      Is bringing near, with smile or tear?
         O, will my hearth be warm,
            My table furnished well?
      Or will my fare be sordid care,
            Another weary spell?

[*Punch*, 22 June 1904]

At Lord's

It is little I repair to the matches of the Southron folk,
  Though my own red roses there may blow;
It is little I repair to the matches of the Southron folk,
  Though the red roses crest the caps, I know.
For the field is full of shades as I near the shadowy coast,
And a ghostly batsman plays to the bowling of a ghost,
And I look through my tears on a soundless-clapping host
  As the run-stealers flicker to and fro,
  To and fro:
O my Hornby and my Barlow long ago!

It is Glo'ster coming North, the irresistible,
  The Shire of the Graces, long ago!
It is Gloucestershire up North, the irresistible,
  And newly-risen Lancashire the foe!
A Shire so young that has scarce impressed its traces,
Ah, how shall it stand before all-resistless Graces?
O, little red rose, their bats are as maces
  To beat thee down, this summer long ago!

This day of seventy-eight they are come up North against thee,
  This day of seventy-eight, long ago!
The champion of the centuries, he cometh up against thee,
  With his brethren, every one a famous foe!
The long-whiskered Doctor, that laugheth rules to scorn,
While the bowler, pitched against him, bans the day that he
  was born;
And G.F. with his science makes the fairest length forlorn;
  They are come from the West to work thee woe!

It is little I repair to the matches of the Southron folk,
  Though my own red roses there may blow;
It is little I repair to the matches of the Southron folk,

Though the red roses crest the caps, I know.
For the field is full of shades as I near the shadowy coast,
And a ghostly batsman plays to the bowling of a ghost,
And I look through my tears on a soundless-clapping host
  As the run-stealers flicker to and fro,
  To and fro:
O my Hornby and my Barlow long ago!

The Massacre

The shadow of a poplar tree
　Lay in that lake of sun,
As I with my little sword went in –
　Against a thousand, one.

Haughty, and infinitely armed,
　Insolent in their wrath,
Plumed high with purple plumes they held
　The narrow meadow path.

The air was sultry; all was still;
　The sun like flashing glass;
And snip-snap my light-whispering steel
　In arcs of light did pass.

Lightly and dull fell each proud head,
　Spiked keen without avail,
Till swam my uncontented blade
　With ichor green and pale.

And silence fell: the rushing sun
　Stood still in paths of heat,
Gazing in waves of horror on
　The dead about my feet.

Never a whir of wing, no bee
　Stirred o'er the shameful slain;
Nought but a thirsty wasp crept in
　Stooped, and came out again.

The very air trembled in fear;
　Eclipsing shadow seemed
Rising in crimson waves of gloom –
　On one who dreamed.

The Sons of Martha

The Sons of Mary seldom bother, for they have inherited that good
  part;
But the Sons of Martha favour their Mother of the careful soul and
  the troubled heart.
And because she lost her temper once, and because she was rude
  to the Lord her Guest,
Her Sons must wait upon Mary's Sons, world without end,
  reprieve, or rest.

It is their care in all the ages to take the buffet and cushion
  the shock.
It is their care that the gear engages; it is their care that the
  switches lock.
It is their care that the wheels run truly; it is their care to embark
  and entrain,
Tally, transport, and deliver duly the Sons of Mary by land
  and main.

They say to mountains, 'Be ye removèd.' They say to the lesser
  floods, 'Be dry.'
Under their rods are the rocks reprovèd – they are not afraid of
  that which is high.
Then do the hill-tops shake to the summit – then is the bed of the
  deep laid bare,
That the Sons of Mary may overcome it, pleasantly sleeping and
  unaware.

They finger death at their gloves' end where they piece and
  repiece the living wires.
He rears against the gates they tend: they feed him hungry behind
  their fires.
Early at dawn, ere men see clear, they stumble into his terrible
  stall,
And hale him forth like a haltered steer, and goad and turn him till
  evenfall.

To these from birth is Belief forbidden; from these till death is
  Relief afar.
They are concerned with matters hidden – under the earth-line
  their altars are –
The secret fountains to follow up, waters withdrawn to restore to
  the mouth,
And gather the floods as in a cup, and pour them again at a city's
  drouth.

They do not preach that their God will rouse them a little before
  the nuts work loose.
They do not teach that His Pity allows them to drop their job when
  they dam'-well choose.
As in the thronged and the lighted ways, so in the dark and the
  desert they stand,
Wary and watchful all their days that their brethren's days may be
  long in the land.

Raise ye the stone or cleave the wood to make a path more fair
  or flat –
Lo, it is black already with blood some Son of Martha spilled
  for that!
Not as a ladder from earth to Heaven, not as a witness to any creed,
But simple service simply given to his own kind in their common
  need.

And the Sons of Mary smile and are blessèd – they know the
  Angels are on their side.
They know in them is the Grace confessèd, and for them are the
  Mercies multiplied.
They sit at the Feet – they hear the Word – they see how truly the
  Promise runs.
They have cast their burden upon the Lord, and – the Lord He lays
  it on Martha's Sons!

A Beggar's Life

When farmers sweat and toil at ploughs,
  The wives give me cool milk and sweet;
When merchants in their office brood,
  Their ladies give me cakes to eat,
And hot tea for my happy blood;
  This is a jolly life indeed,
  To do no work and get my need.

I have no child for future thought,
  I feed no belly but my own,
And I can sleep when toilers fail;
  Content, though sober, sleeps on stone,
But Care can't sleep with down and ale;
  This is a happy life indeed,
  To do no work and get my need.

I trouble not for pauper's grave,
  There is no feeling after death;
The king will be as deaf to praise
  As I to blame – when this world saith
A word of us in after days;
  It is a jolly life indeed,
  To do no work and get my need.

Song for the Twenty-fourth of May

I

The character and strength of us
 Who conquer everywhere,
We sing the English of it thus,
 And bid the world beware:
 We bid the world beware
The perfect heart and will,
 That dare the utmost men may dare
And follow freedom still.
  Sea-room, land-room, ours, my masters, ours,
   Hand in hand with destiny, and first among the Powers!
   Our boasted Ocean Empire, Sirs, we boast of it again,
   Our Monarch, and our Rulers, and our Women, and our Men!

II

The pillars of our Empire stand
 In unforgotten graves;
We build dominion on the land,
 And greatness on the waves:
 Our Empire on the waves,
Established firm and sure,
 And founded deep in Ocean's caves
While honour shall endure.
  Sea-room, land-room, honourably ours,
   Hand in hand with destiny and first among the Powers!
   Our boasted Ocean Empire, Sirs, we boast of it again,
   Our ancient Isles, our Lands afar, and all our loyal Men!

Our flag, on every wind unfurled,
　　Proclaims from sea to sea
A future and a nobler world
　　Where men and thoughts are free:
　　Our men, our thoughts are free:
Our wars are waged for peace:
　　We stand in arms for liberty
Till bonds and bondage cease.
　　　　Sea-room, land-room, ours, appointed ours,
　　　　Conscious of our calling and the first among the Powers!
　　　　Our boasted Ocean Sovereignty, again and yet again!
　　　　Our Counsel, and our Conduct, and our Armaments and Men.

The Ballad of Camden Town

I walked with Maisie long years back
   The streets of Camden Town,
I splendid in my suit of black,
   And she divine in brown.

Hers was a proud and noble face,
   A secret heart, and eyes
Like water in a lonely place
   Beneath unclouded skies.

A bed, a chest, a faded mat,
   And broken chairs a few,
Were all we had to grace our flat
   In Hazel Avenue.

But I could walk to Hampstead Heath,
   And crown her head with daisies,
And watch the streaming world beneath,
   And men with other Maisies.

When I was ill and she was pale
   And empty stood our store,
She left the latchkey on its nail,
   And saw me nevermore.

Perhaps she cast herself away
   Lest both of us should drown:
Perhaps she feared to die, as they
   Who die in Camden Town.

What came of her? The bitter nights
   Destroy the rose and lily,
And souls are lost among the lights
   Of painted Piccadilly.

What came of her? The river flows
   So deep and wide and stilly,
And waits to catch the fallen rose
   And clasp the broken lily.

I dream she dwells in London still
   And breathes the evening air,
And often walk to Primrose Hill,
   And hope to meet her there.

Once more together we will live,
   For I will find her yet:
I have so little to forgive;
   So much, I can't forget.

Divorce

A voice from the dark is calling me.
In the close house I nurse a fire.
Out in the dark, cold winds rush free,
To the rock heights of my desire.
I smother in the house in the valley below,
Let me out to the night, let me go, let me go!

Spirits that ride the sweeping blast,
Frozen in rigid tenderness,
Wait! For I leave the fire at last,
My little-love's warm loneliness.
I smother in the house in the valley below,
Let me out to the night, let me go, let me go!

High on the hills are beating drums.
Clear from a line of marching men
To the rock's edge the hero comes.
He calls me, and he calls again.
On the hill there is fighting, victory, or quick death,
In the house is the fire, which I fan with sick breath.
I smother in the house in the valley below,
Let me out to the dark, let me go, let me go!

'Oh! who are these in scant array?'

Oh! who are these in scant array
Whom we behold at break of day;
Strange their attire! oh, who are they?
  The Suffragettes in Holloway.

And who are these when chapel's done
Stream out beneath an April sun,
To laugh and jump or shout and run?
  The Suffragettes in Holloway.

Who is it say in tones which freeze,
'Pass on this way, convicted, please;
Don't dare to think or breathe or sneeze?'
  The Wardresses in Holloway.

And who is he, tho' grand his air,
Doffs not his hat to ladies fair?
Is it because he has no hair?
  The Governor in Holloway.

Then whilst we eat our frugal food,
Who breaks upon our solitude,
And says, 'You're all so beastly rude'?
  Why 'Mother's own' in Holloway.

And who, with sanctimonious drone,
Tells tales of highly moral tone,
Whilst gazing upwards at the dome?
  The Chaplain, sure, in Holloway.

Hark! who is this with stealthy tread,
Comes round each day to count his dead,
And scalps his victims, so 'tis said?
  The Doctor, in grim Holloway.

But who is this now comes in view,
His smiling face cheers others too?
Father McCarroll, 'here's to you,'
   The only *Man* in Holloway.

But there is one we'll ne'er forget,
She says she's not – and yet and yet
We feel she *is* a Suffragette?
   The Matron dear, of Holloway.

A Song of Swords

'A drove of cattle came into a village called Swords, and was stopped by
the rioters.' Daily Paper

In the place called Swords on the Irish road
It is told for a new renown
How we held the horns of the cattle, and how
We will hold the horns of the devil now
Ere the lord of hell, with the horn on his brow,
   Is crowned in Dublin town.

Light in the East and light in the West,
And light on the cruel lords,
On the souls that suddenly all men knew,
And the green flag flew and the red flag flew,
And many a wheel of the world stopped too,
   When the cattle were stopped at Swords.

Be they sinners or less than saints
That smite in the street for rage,
We know where the shame shines bright; we know
You that they smite at, you their foe,
Lords of the lawless wage and low,
   This is your lawful wage.

You pinched a child to a torture price
That you dared not name in words;
So black a jest was the silver bit
That your own speech shook for the shame of it,
And the coward was plain as a cow they hit
   When the cattle have strayed at Swords.

The wheel of the torment of wives went round
To break men's brotherhood;
You gave the good Irish blood to grease

The clubs of your country's enemies;
You saw the brave man beat to the knees:
  And you saw that it was good.

The rope of the rich is long and long –
The longest of hangmen's cords;
But the kings and crowds are holding their breath,
In a giant shadow o'er all beneath
Where God stands holding the scales of Death
  Between the cattle and Swords.

Haply the lords that hire and lend,
The lowest of all men's lords,
Who sell their kind like kine at a fair,
Will find no head of their cattle there;
But faces of men where cattle were:
  Faces of men – and Swords.

And the name shining and terrible,
The sternest of all man's words,
Still marks that place to seek or shun,
In the streets where the struggling cattle run –
Grass and a silence of judgment done
  In the place that is called Swords.

1914: *Peace*

Now, God be thanked Who has matched us with His hour,
   And caught our youth, and wakened us from sleeping,
With hand made sure, clear eye, and sharpened power,
   To turn, as swimmers into cleanness leaping,
Glad from a world grown old and cold and weary,
   Leave the sick hearts that honour could not move,
And half-men, and their dirty songs and dreary,
   And all the little emptiness of love!

Oh! we, who have known shame, we have found release there,
   Where there's no ill, no grief, but sleep has mending,
     Naught broken save this body, lost but breath;
Nothing to shake the laughing heart's long peace there
   But only agony, and that has ending;
     And the worst friend and enemy is but Death.

'This is No Case of Petty Right or Wrong'

This is no case of petty right or wrong
That politicians or philosophers
Can judge. I hate not Germans, nor grow hot
With love of Englishmen, to please newspapers.
Beside my hate for one fat patriot
My hatred of the Kaiser is love true: –
A kind of god he is, banging a gong.
But I have not to choose between the two,
Or between justice and injustice. Dinned
With war and argument I read no more
Than in the storm smoking along the wind
Athwart the wood. Two witches' cauldrons roar.
From one the weather shall rise clear and gay;
Out of the other an England beautiful
And like her mother that died yesterday.
Little I know or care if, being dull,
I shall miss something that historians
Can rake out of the ashes when perchance
The phœnix broods serene above their ken.
But with the best and meanest Englishmen
I am one in crying, God save England, lest
We lose what never slaves and cattle blessed.
The ages made her that made us from dust:
She is all we know and live by, and we trust
She is good and must endure, loving her so:
And as we love ourselves we hate her foe.

'The General inspecting the trenches'

The General inspecting the trenches
Exclaimed with a horrified shout,
'I refuse to command a Division
Which leaves its excreta about.'

But nobody took any notice
No one was prepared to refute,
That the presence of shit was congenial
Compared with the presence of Shute.

And certain responsible critics
Made haste to reply to his words
Observing that his Staff advisers
Consisted entirely of turds.

For shit may be shot at odd corners
And paper supplied there to suit,
But a shit would be shot without mourners
If somebody shot that shit Shute.

The Effect

'The effect of our bombardment was terrific. One man told me he had
never seen so many dead before.' War Correspondent

'*He'd never seen so many dead before.*'
They sprawled in yellow daylight while he swore
And gasped and lugged his everlasting load
Of bombs along what once had been a road.
'*How peaceful are the dead.*'
Who put that silly gag in someone's head?

'*He'd never seen so many dead before.*'
The lilting words danced up and down his brain,
While corpses jumped and capered in the rain.
No, no; he wouldn't count them any more...
The dead have done with pain:
They've choked; they can't come back to life again.

When Dick was killed last week he looked like that,
Flapping along the fire-step like a fish,
After the blazing crump had knocked him flat...
'*How many dead? As many as ever you wish.*
Don't count 'em; they're too many.
Who'll buy my nice fresh corpses, two a penny?'

Summer 1917 (Hindenburg Line material)

Spring Offensive

Halted against the shade of a last hill
They fed, and eased of pack-loads, were at ease;
And leaning on the nearest chest or knees
Carelessly slept.
                    But many there stood still
To face the stark blank sky beyond the ridge,
Knowing their feet had come to the end of the world.
Marvelling they stood, and watched the long grass swirled
By the May breeze, murmurous with wasp and midge;
And though the summer oozed into their veins
Like an injected drug for their bodies' pains,
Sharp on their souls hung the imminent ridge of grass,
Fearfully flashed the sky's mysterious glass.

Hour after hour they ponder the warm field
And the far valley behind, where buttercups
Had blessed with gold their slow boots coming up;
When even the little brambles would not yield
But clutched and clung to them like sorrowing arms.
[All their strange day] they breathe like trees unstirred.

Till like a cold gust thrills the little word
At which each body and its soul begird
And tighten them for battle. No alarms
Of bugles, no high flags, no clamorous haste, –
Only a lift and flare of eyes that faced
The sun, like a friend with whom their love is done.
O larger shone that smile against the sun, –
Mightier than his whose bounty these have spurned.

So, soon they topped the hill, and raced together
Over an open stretch of herb and heather
Exposed. And instantly the whole sky burned

With fury against them; earth set sudden cups
In thousands for their blood; and the green slope
Chasmed and deepened sheer to infinite space.

Of them who running on that last high place
Breasted the surf of bullets, or went up
On the hot blast and fury of hell's upsurge,
Or plunged and fell away past this world's verge,
Some say God caught them even before they fell.

But what say such as from existence' brink
Ventured but drave too swift to sink,
The few who rushed in the body to enter hell,
And there out-fiending all its fiends and flames
With superhuman inhumanities,
Long-famous glories, immemorial shames –
And crawling slowly back, have by degrees
Regained cool peaceful air in wonder –
Why speak not they of comrades that went under?

from *Hugh Selwyn Mauberley*

IV

These fought in any case,
and some believing,
               pro domo, in any case...
Some quick to arm,
some for adventure,
some from fear of weakness,
some from fear of censure,
some for love of slaughter, in imagination,
learning later...
some in fear, learning love of slaughter;

Died some, pro patria,
          non 'dulce' non 'et decor'...

walked eye-deep in hell
believing in old men's lies, then unbelieving
came home, home to a lie,
home to many deceits,
home to old lies and new infamy;
usury age-old and age-thick
and liars in public places.

Daring as never before, wastage as never before.
Young blood and high blood,
fair cheeks, and fine bodies;

fortitude as never before

frankness as never before,
disillusions as never told in the old days,
hysterias, trench confessions,
laughter out of dead bellies.

V

There died a myriad,
And of the best, among them,
For an old bitch gone in the teeth,
For a botched civilization,

Charm, smiling at the good mouth,
Quick eyes gone under earth's lid,

For two gross of broken statues,
For a few thousand battered books.

The Second Coming

Turning and turning in the widening gyre
The falcon cannot hear the falconer;
Things fall apart; the centre cannot hold;
Mere anarchy is loosed upon the world,
The blood-dimmed tide is loosed, and everywhere
The ceremony of innocence is drowned;
The best lack all conviction, while the worst
Are full of passionate intensity,

Surely some revelation is at hand;
Surely the Second Coming is at hand.
The Second Coming! Hardly are those words out
When a vast image out of *Spiritus Mundi*
Troubles my sight: somewhere in sands of the desert
A shape with lion body and the head of a man,
A gaze blank and pitiless as the sun,
Is moving its slow thighs; while all about it
Reel shadows of the indignant desert birds.
The darkness drops again, but now I know
That twenty centuries of stony sleep
Were vexed to nightmare by a rocking cradle,
And what rough beast, its hour come round at last,
Slouches towards Bethlehem to be born?

Saturday Market

Bury your heart in some deep green hollow
  Or hide it up in a kind old tree
Better still, give it the swallow
  When she goes over the sea.

In Saturday Market there's eggs a 'plenty
  And dead-alive ducks with their legs tied down,
Grey old gaffers and boys of twenty –
  Girls and the women of the town –
Pitchers and sugar-sticks, ribbons and laces,
  Posies and whips and dicky-birds' seed,
Silver pieces and smiling faces,
  In Saturday Market they've all they need.

What were you showing in Saturday Market
  That set it grinning from end to end
Girls and gaffers and boys of twenty – ?
  Cover it close with your shawl, my friend –
Hasten you home with the laugh behind you,
  Over the down –, out of sight,
Fasten your door, though no one will find you,
  No one will look on a Market night.

See, you, the shawl is wet, take out from under
  The red dead thing –. In the white of the moon
On the flags does it stir again? Well, and no wonder!
  Best make an end of it; bury it soon.
If there is blood on the hearth who'll know it?
  Or blood on the stairs,
When a murder is over and done why show it?
  In Saturday Market nobody cares.

Then lie you straight on your bed for a short, short weeping
   And still, for a long, long rest,
There's never a one in the town so sure of sleeping
   As you, in the house on the down with a hole in your breast.

  Think no more of the swallow,
    Forget, you, the sea,
Never again remember the deep green hollow
    Or the top of the kind old tree!

Eight O'Clock

He stood, and heard the steeple
  Sprinkle the quarters on the morning town.
One, two, three, four, to market-place and people
  It tossed them down.

Strapped, noosed, nighing his hour,
  He stood and counted them and cursed his luck;
And then the clock collected in the tower
  Its strength, and struck.

Ballade of Genuine Concern

A child at Brighton has been left to drown:
  A railway train has jumped the line at Crewe:
I haven't got the change for half a crown:
  I can't imagine what on earth to do...
  Three bisons have stampeded from the Zoo.
A German fleet has anchored in the Clyde.
  By God the wretched country's up the flue!
– The ice is breaking up on every side.

What! Further news? Rhodesian stocks are down?
  England, my England, can the news be true!
Cannot the Duke be got to come to town?
  Or will not Mr Hooper pull us through?
  And now the Bank is stopping payment too,
The chief cashier has cut his throat and died,
  And Scotland Yard has failed to find a clue:
– The ice is breaking up on every side.

A raging mob inflamed by Charley Brown
  Is tearing up the rails of Waterloo;
They've hanged the Chancellor in wig and gown,
  The Speaker, and the Chief Inspector too!
  Police! Police! Is this the road to Kew?
I can't keep up: my garter's come untied:
  I shall be murdered by the savage crew.
– The ice is breaking up on every side.

Envoi

  Prince of the Empire, Prince of Timbuctoo,
Prince eight feet round and nearly four feet wide,
  Do try to run a little faster, do.
– The ice is breaking up on every side.

Old Tale

If one's heart is broken twenty times a day,
What easier thing to fling the bits away,
But still one gathers fragments, and looks for wire,
Or patches it up like some old bicycle tyre.

Bicycle tyres fare hardly on roads, but the heart
Has a longer time than rubber, they sheath a cart
With iron; so lumbering and slow my mind must be made –
To bother the heart and to teach things and learn it its trade.

The Hollow Men

A penny for the Old Guy

I

We are the hollow men
We are the stuffed men
Leaning together
Headpiece filled with straw. Alas!
Our dried voices, when
We whisper together
Are quiet and meaningless
As wind in dry grass
Or rats' feet over broken glass
In our dry cellar

Shape without form, shade without colour,
Paralysed force, gesture without motion;

Those who have crossed
With direct eyes, to death's other Kingdom
Remember us – if at all – not as lost
Violent souls, but only
As the hollow men
The stuffed men.

II

Eyes I dare not meet in dreams
In death's dream kingdom
These do not appear:
There, the eyes are
Sunlight on a broken column
There, is a tree swinging
And voices are
In the wind's singing

More distant and more solemn
Than a fading star.

Let me be no nearer
In death's dream kingdom
Let me also wear
Such deliberate disguises
Rat's coat, crowskin, crossed staves
In a field
Behaving as the wind behaves
No nearer –

Not that final meeting
In the twilight kingdom

III

This is the dead land
This is cactus land
Here the stone images
Are raised, here they receive
The supplication of a dead man's hand
Under the twinkle of a fading star.

Is it like this
In death's other kingdom
Waking alone
At the hour when we are
Trembling with tenderness
Lips that would kiss
Form prayers to broken stone.

IV

The eyes are not here
There are no eyes here
In this valley of dying stars
In this hollow valley
This broken jaw of our lost kingdoms

In this last of meeting places
We grope together

And avoid speech
Gathered on this beach of the tumid river

Sightless, unless
The eyes reappear
As the perpetual star
Multifoliate rose
Of death's twilight kingdom
The hope only
Of empty men.

V

Here we go round the prickly pear
Prickly pear prickly pear
Here we go round the prickly pear
At five o'clock in the morning.

Between the idea
And the reality
Between the motion
And the act
Falls the Shadow

For Thine is the Kingdom

Between the conception
And the creation
Between the emotion
And the response
Falls the Shadow

Life is very long

Between the desire
And the spasm
Between the potency
And the existence
Between the essence
And the descent
Falls the Shadow

For Thine is the Kingdom

For Thine is
Life is
For Thine is the

This is the way the world ends
This is the way the world ends
This is the way the world ends
Not with a bang but a whimper.

'Do you remember 1926?'

Do you remember 1926? That summer of soups and speeches,
The sunlight on the idle wheels and the deserted crossings,
And the laughter and the cursing in the moonlit streets?
Do you remember 1926? The slogans and the penny concerts,
The jazz-bands and the moorland picnics,
And the slanderous tongues of famous cities?
Do you remember 1926? The great dream and the swift disaster,
The fanatic and the traitor, and more than all,
The bravery of the simple, faithful folk?
'Ay, ay, we remember 1926,' said Dai and Shinkin,
As they stood on the kerb in Charing Cross Road,
'And we shall remember 1926 until our blood is dry.'

Midnight Lamentation

When you and I go down
Breathless and cold,
Our faces both worn back
To earthly mould,
How lonely we shall be;
What shall we do,
You without me,
I without you?

I cannot bear the thought
You, first, may die,
Nor of how you will weep
Should I.
We are too much alone;
What can we do
To make our bodies one:
You, me; I, you?

We are most nearly born
Of one same kind;
We have the same delight,
The same true mind,
Must we then part, we part;
Is there no way
To keep a beating heart,
And light of day?

I could now rise and run
Through street on street
To where you are breathing – you,
That we might meet,
And that your living voice
Might sound above
Fear, and we two rejoice
Within our love.

How frail the body is,
And we are made
As only in decay
To lean and fade.
I think too much of death;
There is a gloom
When I can't hear your breath
Calm in some room.

O, but how suddenly
Either may droop;
Countenance be so white,
Body stoop.
Then there may be a place
Where fading flowers
Drop on a lifeless face
Through weeping hours.

Is then nothing safe?
Can we not find
Some everlasting life
In our one mind?
I feel it like disgrace
Only to understand
Your spirit through your word,
Or by your hand.

I cannot find a way
Through love and through;
I cannot reach beyond
Body, to you.
When you or I must go
Down evermore,
There'll be no more to say
– But a locked door.

Luxury

The long, sleek cars rasp softly on the kerb
and chattering women rise from cushioned nests,
flamingo-tall, whose coral legs disturb
the mirror-surface where creation rests.

Aconite, Opium, Mandragora, Girl!
Essential phials exquisite array!
Poisons whose frail, consumptive fervours whirl
the stony city to a fierce decay.

The churches' sun-dried clay crumbles at last,
the Courts of Justice wither like a stink
and honourable statues melt as fast
as greasy garbage down a kitchen-sink.

Commercial palaces, hotels de luxe
and Banks in white, immutable ravines,
life's skeleton unfleshed by cynic rooks,
remain to warn the traveller what it means.

The shady universe, once haunt of play,
in leafless winter bares its ways of stone;
the paths we shared, the mounds on which we lay
were ruled by Time and lifted by old bone.

Time has no pity for this world of graves
nor for its dead decked out in feathery shrouds.
The ghoul must perish with the flesh he craves
when stars' hoarse bells of doom toll in the clouds.

Change of Government

We've got a change of government
if you know what I mean.
Auntie Maud has come to keep house
instead of Aunt Gwendoline.

They say that Auntie Maud, you know,
is rather common; she's not
so well brought up as Aunt Gwendoline is,
so perhaps she'll be more on the spot.

That's what we hope: we hope she'll be
a better manager: for Oh dear me
Aunt Gwen was a poor one! but Aunt Maud, you see
was brought up poor, so she'll *have* to be

more careful. Though if she's not
won't it be awful! what shall we do?
Aunt Libby's really a feeble lot,
and I simply daren't think of Aunt Lou!

I've never seen her, but they say
she's a holy terror: she takes your best frock
and *all* your best things, and just gives them away
to the char, who's as good as you are, any day.

And she makes you go to work, even if
you've got money of your own.
And she shuts you in the cellar for the least little tiff,
and just loves to hear you sob and groan.

Oh I do hope Aunt Maud will manage all right!
Because they say, if she doesn't
Aunt Louie is almost bound to come
with all our horrible cousins

that we've never seen, coming stamping and swearing
and painting the wood-work red
just to show how dangerous they are!
Oh, Aunt Louie's the one *I* dread.

Song: *Lift-Boy*

Let me tell you the story of how I began:
I began as the boot-boy and ended as the boot-man,
With nothing in my pockets but a jack-knife and a button,
With nothing in my pockets but a jack-knife and a button,
With nothing in my pockets.

Let me tell you the story of how I went on:
I began as the lift-boy and ended as the lift-man,
With nothing in my pockets but a jack-knife and a button,
With nothing in my pockets but a jack-knife and a button,
With nothing in my pockets.

I found it very easy to whistle and play
With nothing in my head or my pockets all day,
With nothing in my pockets.

But along came Old Eagle, like Moses or David;
He stopped at the fourth floor and preached me Damnation:
'Not a soul shall be savèd, not one shall be savèd.
The whole First Creation shall forfeit salvation:
From knife-boy to lift-boy, from ragged to regal,
Not one shall be savèd, not you, not Old Eagle,
No soul on earth escapeth, even if all repent –'
So I cut the cords of the lift and down we went,
With nothing in our pockets.

Aus Dem Zweiten Reich

I

Women swarm in Tauentsienstrasse.
Clients of Nollendorferplatz cafés,
shadows on sweaty glass,
hum, drum on the table
    to the negerband's faint jazz.
Humdrum at the table.

Hour and hour
meeting against me,
efficiently whipped cream,
efficiently metropolitan chatter and snap,
transparent glistening wrapper
    for a candy pack.

Automatic, somewhat too clean,
body and soul similarly scented,
on time,
rapid, dogmatic, automatic and efficient,
ganz modern.

'Sturm über Asien' is off, some other flicker...
Kiss me in the taxi, twist fingers in the dark.
A box of chocolates is necessary.
I am preoccupied with Sie and Du.
    The person on the screen,
divorced and twenty-five, must pass for fourteen
for the story's sake, an insipidity
contrived to dress her in shorts
and a widenecked shirt with nothing underneath
so that you see her small breasts when she
often bends towards the camera.
Audience mainly male stirs,
    I am teased too,

I like this public blonde better than my brunette,
　　but that will never do.
– Let's go,
arm in arm on foot over gleaming snow
past the Gedächtnis Kirche
to the loud crowded cafés near the Bahnhof Zoo.

Better hugged together ('to keep warm')
under street trees whimpering to the keen wind
over snow whispering to many feet,
find out a consolingly mediocre
neighbourhood without music, varnished faces
bright and sagacious against varnished walls,
youngsters red from skating,
businessmen reading the papers:
no need to talk – much:
what indolence supplies.
'If, smoothing this silk skirt, you pinch my thighs,
that will be fabelhaft'.

II

Herr Lignitz knows Old Berlin. It is near the Post Office
with several rather disorderly public houses.
'You have no naked pictures in your English magazines.
It is shocking. Berlin is very shocking to the English. Are you
　　shocked?
Would you like to see the naked cabarets
in Jaegerstrasse? I think there is
nothing like that in Paris.
Or a department store? They are said to be
almost equal to Macy's in America.'

III

The renowned author of
more plays than Shakespeare
stopped and did his hair
with a pocket glass
before entering the village,

afraid they wouldn't recognize
caricature and picturepostcard,
that windswept chevelure.

Who talked about poetry,
and he said nothing at all;
plays,
and he said nothing at all;
politics,
and he stirred as if a flea
bit him
but wouldnt let on in company;
and the frost in Berlin,
muttered: 𝔖𝔠𝔥𝔯𝔢𝔠𝔨𝔩𝔦𝔠𝔥

Viennese bow from the hips,
notorieties
contorted laudatory lips,
wreaths and bouquets surround
the mindless menopause.
Stillborn fecundities,
frostbound applause.

The Express

After the first powerful, plain manifesto
The black statement of pistons, without more fuss
But gliding like a queen, she leaves the station.
Without bowing and with restrained unconcern
She passes the houses which humbly crowd outside,
The gasworks, and at last the heavy page
Of death, printed by gravestones in the cemetery.
Beyond the town, there lies the open country
Where, gathering speed, she acquires mystery,
The luminous self-possession of ships on ocean.
It is now she begins to sing – at first quite low
Then loud, and at last with a jazzy madness –
The song of her whistle screaming at curves,
Of deafening tunnels, brakes, innumerable bolts.
And always light, aerial, underneath
Retreats the elate metre of her wheels.
Steaming through metal landscape on her lines,
She plunges new eras of white happiness,
Where speed throws up strange shapes, broad curves
And parallels clean like trajectories from guns.
At last, further than Edinburgh or Rome,
Beyond the crest of the world, she reaches night
Where only a low stream-line brightness
Of phosphorus on the tossing hills is light.
Ah, like a comet through flame, she moves entranced,
Wrapt in her music no bird song, no, nor bough
Breaking with honey buds, shall ever equal.

The Midsummer Apple Tree

Comrade, comrade, come away
Down to Midsummer apple bough.
Who you are, I can scarcely say,
Only know you are here and now
Under the Midsummer apple bough

Here's the apple for us to share
Under the Midsummer apple tree.
Priests and schools have said, beware,
Shame and sin and death, all three
Hang from the Midsummer apple tree

Comrade, comrade, these are lies!
Under the Midsummer apple leaves
I can tell you and I am wise:
We are neither brutes nor thieves
Here in the Midsummer apple leaves

What we want we both shall get
Under the holy apple tree:
Eat our cake and have it yet,
Schools and priests must let us free,

All our devils be overset,
Here where the hay is sweet and wet,
I like you and you like me
Under the Midsummer apple tree.

A Bride in the 30's

Easily, my dear, you move, easily your head
And easily as through the leaves of a photograph album I'm led
Through the night's delights and the day's impressions,
Past the tall tenements and the trees in the wood;
Though sombre the sixteen skies of Europe
    And the Danube flood.

Looking and loving our behaviours pass
The stones, the steels and the polished glass;
Lucky to Love the new pansy railway,
The sterile farms where his looks are fed,
And in the policed unlucky city
    Lucky his bed.

He from these lands of terrifying mottoes
Makes worlds as innocent as Beatrix Potter's;
Through bankrupt countries where they mend the roads
Along the endless plains his will is
Intent as a collector to pursue
    His greens and lilies.

Easy for him to find in your face
The pool of silence and the tower of grace,
To conjure a camera into a wishing rose;
Simple to excite in the air from a glance
The horses, the fountains, the sidedrum, the trombone
    And the dance, the dance.

Summoned by such a music from our time,
Such images to audience come
As vanity cannot dispel nor bless:
Hunger and love in their variations
Grouped invalids watching the flight of the birds
    And single assassins.

Ten thousand of the desperate marching by
Five feet, six feet, seven feet high:
Hitler and Mussolini in their wooing poses
Churchill acknowledging the voters' greeting
Roosevelt at the microphone, Van der Lubbe laughing
      And our first meeting.

But love, except at our proposal,
Will do no trick at his disposal;
Without opinions of his own, performs
The programme that we think of merit,
And through our private stuff must work
      His public spirit.

Certain it became while we were still incomplete
There were certain prizes for which we would never compete;
A choice was killed by every childish illness,
The boiling tears among the hothouse plants,
The rigid promise fractured in the garden,
      And the long aunts.

And every day there bolted from the field
Desires to which we could not yield;
Fewer and clearer grew the plans,
Schemes for a life and sketches for a hatred,
And early among my interesting scrawls
      Appeared your portrait.

You stand now before me, flesh and bone
These ghosts would like to make their own.
Are they your choices? O, be deaf
When hatred would proffer her immediate pleasure
And glory swap her fascinating rubbish
      For your one treasure.

Be deaf too, standing uncertain now,
A pine tree shadow across your brow,
To what I hear and wish I did not:
The voice of love saying lightly, brightly –
'Be Lubbe, Be Hitler, but be my good
      Daily, nightly.'

The power that corrupts, that power to excess
The beautiful quite naturally possess:
To them the fathers and the children turn:
And all who long for their destruction,
The arrogant and self-insulted, wait
 The looked instruction.

Shall idleness ring then your eyes like the pest?
O will you unnoticed and mildly like the rest,
Will you join the lost in their sneering circles,
Forfeit the beautiful interest and fall
Where the engaging face is the face of the betrayer
 And the pang is all?

Wind shakes the tree; the mountains darken;
And the heart repeats though we would not hearken
'Yours is the choice, to whom the gods awarded
The language of learning and the language of love
Crooked to move as a moneybug or a cancer
 Or straight as a dove.'

After Two Thousand Years

The Christians have had two thousand years
  And what have they done? –
Made the bloodiest and beastliest world ever seen
  Under the sun.

No Christian refuses to profit himself
  From his brother's misfortune.
The devil who would sup with our Christian banks
  Must sup with a hellish long spoon.

The Christian Churches are all built up
  In utter defiance of all Christ taught.
Co-religionists war at home and abroad,
  Each side supported by the self-same God.

And blandly the Bishops bestow their blessings
  On any murderer or fraud with the wit
To pay them, lip-serve the Cross, and keep
  The working-classes carrying it.

A Letter from Aragon

This is a quiet sector of a quiet front.

We buried Ruiz in a new pine coffin,
But the shroud was too small and his washed feet stuck out.
The stink of his corpse came through the clean pine boards
And some of the bearers wrapped handkerchiefs round
    their faces.
Death was not dignified.
We hacked a ragged grave in the unfriendly earth
And fired a ragged volley over the grave.

You could tell from our listlessness, no one much missed him.

This is a quiet sector of a quiet front.
There is no poison gas and no H. E.

But when they shelled the other end of the village
And the streets were choked with dust
Women came screaming out of the crumbling houses,
Clutched under one arm the naked rump of an infant.
I thought: how ugly fear is.

This is a quiet sector of a quiet front.
Our nerves are steady; we all sleep soundly.

In the clean hospital bed, my eyes were so heavy
Sleep easily blotted out one ugly picture,
A wounded militiaman moaning on a stretcher,
Now out of danger, but still crying for water,
Strong against death, but unprepared for such pain.

This on a quiet front.

But when I shook hands to leave, an Anarchist worker
Said: 'Tell the workers of England
This was a war not of our own making,
We did not seek it.
But if ever the Fascists again rule Barcelona
It will be as a heap of ruins with us workers beneath it.'

Missing Dates

Slowly the poison the whole blood stream fills.
It is not the effort nor the failure tires.
The waste remains, the waste remains and kills.

It is not your system or clear sight that mills
Down small to the consequence a life requires;
Slowly the poison the whole blood stream fills.

They bled an old dog dry yet the exchange rills
Of young dog blood gave but a month's desires
The waste remains, the waste remains and kills.

It is the Chinese tombs and the slag hills
Usurp the soil, and not the soil retires.
Slowly the poison the whole blood stream fills.

Not to have fire is to be a skin that shrills.
The complete fire is death. From partial fires
The waste remains, the waste remains and kills.

It is the poems you have lost, the ills
From missing dates, at which the heart expires.
Slowly the poison the whole blood stream fills.
The waste remains, the waste remains and kills.

from *Autumn Journal*

Conferences, adjournments, ultimatums,
　　Flights in the air, castles in the air,
The autopsy of treaties, dynamite under the bridges,
　　The end of *laissez faire*.
After the warm days the rain comes pimpling
　　The paving stones with white
And with the rain the national conscience, creeping,
　　Seeping through the night.
And in the sodden park on Sunday protest
　　Meetings assemble not, as so often, now
Merely to advertise some patent panacea
　　But simply to avow
The need to hold the ditch; a bare avowal
　　That may perhaps imply
Death at the doors in a week but perhaps in the long run
　　Exposure of the lie.
Think of a number, double it, treble it, square it,
　　And sponge it out
And repeat *ad lib.* and mark the slate with crosses;
　　There is no time to doubt
If the puzzle really has an answer. Hitler yells on the wireless,
　　The night is damp and still
And I hear dull blows on wood outside my window;
　　They are cutting down the trees on Primrose Hill.
The wood is white like the roast flesh of chicken,
　　Each tree falling like a closing fan;
No more looking at the view from seats beneath the branches,
　　Everything is going to plan;
They want the crest of this hill for anti-aircraft,
　　The guns will take the view
And searchlights probe the heavens for bacilli
　　With narrow wands of blue.
And the rain came on as I watched the territorials
　　Sawing and chopping and pulling on ropes like a team

In a village tug-of-war; and I found my dog had vanished
    And thought 'This is the end of the old régime,'
But found the police had got her at St John's Wood station
    And fetched her in the rain and went for a cup
Of coffee to an all-night shelter and heard a taxi-driver
    Say 'It turns me up
When I see these soldiers in lorries' - rumble of tumbrils
    Drums in the trees
Breaking the eardrums of the ravished dryads –
    It turns me up; a coffee, please.
And as I go out I see a windscreen-wiper
    In an empty car
Wiping away like mad and I feel astounded
    That things have gone so far.
And I come back here to my flat and wonder whether
    From now on I need take
The trouble to go out choosing stuff for curtains
    As I don't know anyone to make
Curtains quickly. Rather one should quickly
    Stop the cracks for gas or dig a trench
And take one's paltry measures against the coming
    Of the unknown Uebermensch.
But one – meaning I – is bored, am bored, the issue
    Involving principle but bound in fact
To squander principle in panic and self-deception –
    Accessories after the act,
So that all we foresee is rivers in spate sprouting
    With drowning hands
And men like dead frogs floating till the rivers
    Lose themselves in the sands.
And we who have been brought up to think of 'Gallant Belgium'
    As so much blague
Are now preparing again to essay good through evil
    For the sake of Prague;
And must, we suppose, become uncritical, vindictive,
    And must, in order to beat
The enemy, model ourselves upon the enemy,
    A howling radio for our paraclete.

The night continues wet, the axe keeps falling,
   The hill grows bald and bleak
No longer one of the sights of London but maybe
   We shall have fireworks here by this day week.

A Window in Germany

August 1939

Still the mild shower grows on; amid the drops
The grey gnats loiter or frisk; but we within
Like their sport less. So from my window here,
This ample casement built in the huge old wall
Which even a nunnery might find thick enough,
Barred with old iron branchwork monster-thorned,
I glance into the idle croft below.
I could not find a more familiar scene,
Known from my childhood, known to all my race –
The flagged path from the kitchen of the farm
Into the towsled orchard, plum and pear;
And under boughs of elder and stone sty;
The dog's dish which to-day he half forgets;
The nettles cluttering up the heaps of logs,
The raspberry-canes scrambled on leaning pales:
An English casual scene, which tells at once
Of rural mastery, and of rural ease.
Thus from my window here in Germany
The pleasant yard-scape shows. The world beyond
Is Sunday evening, and deserves its peace,
After the dogged action of the week,
The harvest battle fought into the night
With lanterns steady or marching; on whose heel
Tremendous thunder flamed and gunned for hours,
Bursting from Weser's vast black-wooded hills.
Such hills, such forests, even such confluent storm
Were not in my old haunt; but it is much
To find the kinship of this quiet house,
Where gentlest goodness lives and constant care,
And where, from many a nook, far-sundered ghosts,
To whom my ways mean something, gaze on me.

Naming of Parts

Today we have naming of parts. Yesterday,
We had daily cleaning. And tomorrow morning,
We shall have what to do after firing. But today,
Today we have naming of parts. Japonica
Glistens like coral in all of the neighbouring gardens,
And today we have naming of parts.

This is the lower sling swivel. And this
Is the upper sling swivel, whose use you will see
When you are given your slings. And this is the piling swivel,
Which in your case you have not got. The branches
Hold in the gardens their silent, eloquent gestures,
Which in our case we have not got.

This is the safety catch, which is always released
With an easy flick of the thumb. And please do not let me
See anyone using his finger. You can do it quite easy
If you have any strength in your thumb. The blossoms
Are fragile and motionless, never letting anyone see
Any of them using their finger.

And this you can see is the bolt. The purpose of this
Is to open the breech, as you see. We can slide it
Rapidly backwards and forwards: we call this
Easing the spring. And rapidly backwards and forwards
The early bees are assaulting and fumbling the flowers;
They call it easing the Spring.

They call it easing the Spring: it is perfectly easy
If you have any strength in your thumb: like the bolt,
And the breech, and the cocking-piece, and the point of balance,
Which in our case we have not got, and the almond-blossom
Silent in all of the gardens, the bees going backwards and
    forwards,
For today we have naming of parts.

Among Those Killed in the Dawn Raid was a Man Aged a Hundred

When the morning was waking over the war
He put on his clothes and stepped out and he died,
The locks yawned loose and a blast blew them wide,
He dropped where he loved on the burst pavement stone
And the funeral grains of the slaughtered floor.
Tell his street on its back he stopped a sun
And the craters of his eyes grew springshoots and fire
When all the keys shot from the locks, and rang.
Dig no more for the chains of his grey-haired heart.
The heavenly ambulance drawn by a wound
Assembling waits for the spade's ring on the cage.
O keep his bones away from that common cart,
The morning is flying on the wings of his age
And a hundred storks perch on the sun's right hand.

Survivors

With the ship burning in their eyes
The white faces float like refuse
In the darkness – the water screwing
Oily circles where the hot steel lies.

They clutch with fingers frozen into claws
The lifebelts thrown from a destroyer,
And see, between the future's doors,
The gasping entrance of the sea.

Taken on board as many as lived, who
Had a mind left for living and the ocean,
They open eyes running with surf,
Heavy with the grey ghosts of explosion.

The meaning is not yet clear,
Where daybreak died in the smile –
And the mouth remained stiff
And grinning, stupid for a while.

But soon they joke, easy and warm,
As men will who have died once
Yet somehow were able to find their way –
Muttering this was not included in their pay.

Later, sleepless at night, the brain spinning
With cracked images, they won't forget
The confusion and the oily dead,
Nor yet the casual knack of living.

Sportsmen

'I think I am becoming a God.'

The noble horse with courage in his eye,
clean in the bone, looks up at a shellburst:
away fly the images of the shires
but he puts the pipe back in his mouth.

Peter was unfortunately killed by an 88;
it took his leg off; he died in the ambulance.
When I saw him crawling, he said:
It's most unfair, they've shot my foot off.

How then can I live among this gentle
obsolescent breed of heroes, and not weep?
Unicorns, almost. For they are fading into two legends
in which their stupidity and chivalry are celebrated;
the fool and the hero will be immortals.

These plains were a cricket pitch
and in the hills the tremendous drop fences
brought down some of the runners, who
under these stones and earth lounge still
in famous attitudes of unconcern. Listen
against the bullet cries the simple horn.

Tunisia [May–June] 1943

Rhine Jump, *1944*

They dropped us on the guns, left us in a flaring
lurch of slipstream kicking like sprayed flies, –
till canopies shook sudden heads, inhaled, held a breath, –
alive again we slanted down,
too many, into their doomed sights.

One scrambled moment it was red, green,
dragging to the door of the Douglas then
falling through a monstrous aviary roof
on Guy Fawkes Night (only this was day)
into shrill scarifying glory...

then Germany, the Fatherland, a zooming field –
banged down on it, stood up among the chaos, with
fingers flopped like rubber gloves trying
to slap one's box, slough the afterbirth of chute,
make somehow that snatch of wood.

There were chutes already in those trees, caught:
battalion boys who'd dropped too late or drifted...
harness-ravelled, cocooned there –
like silkworms, moveless, wet...
so easy, against all that white.

But not so many resistive earthworms –
the early birds had seen to that.
Soon, it was rendezvous: a stodgy farm.
The war was folding: fight-thin.
Prisoners happened; columned, toneless.

Next day it was hearing tales again,
having a kip in a pigsty, scouting the dropping-zone
to get silk (knickers for sweethearts, wives);
maybe a green envelope, speculation
about leave, Japan.

Oh and a gun-pit by the way, an 88:
bodiless, nothing special, –
only the pro's interest in other's kit:
grey slacks for the use of, old, ersatz;
with a brown inside stripe: non-ersatz.

Day of Liberation, Bergen–Belsen, May 1945

We build our own prison walls
but that day the doors fell open,
it was holiday time
in the death camp.

Lift him with courtesy,
this silent survivor.
Battle-dress doctors,
we took him from the truck
and put him to bed.

The moving skeleton
had crippled hands,
his skinny palms held secrets:
when I undid the joints I found
five wheat grains huddled there.
In the faces of other people
I witness my distress.

I close my eyes:
ten thousand wasted people
still piled in the flesh-pits.
Death of one is the death of all.
It is not the dead I pity.

R. S. THOMAS   1946

The Village

Scarcely a street, too few houses
To merit the title; just a way between
The one tavern and the one shop
That leads nowhere and fails at the top
Of the short hill, eaten away
By long erosion of the green tide
Of grass creeping perpetually nearer
This last outpost of time past.

So little happens; the black dog
Cracking his fleas in the hot sun
Is history. Yet the girl who crosses
From door to door moves to a scale
Beyond the bland day's two dimensions.

Stay, then, village, for round you spins
On slow axis a world as vast
And meaningful as any poised
By great Plato's solitary mind.

The Body's Independence

I

Father Bianchi taught biology
in Bombay's Don Bosco High School, but skipped
the arts I had learnt about already.
The classroom beamed faces, keen and tight-lipped,
bare brown arms on desks, fingers steady.

His white cassock arm-sleeves rolled against heat,
the Father went through the motions of the body
with a cane to point at a chart and hit
on our heads. His voice, a lesson in prosody,
told us of the secrets of the heart.

He demonstrated man, the button at his throat
loose: he described in the air, with his cane,
the nervous system, showed how the brain was alert.
We furtively laughed at the shape of man,
but his eyes saw further than the chart.

II

A hawk stood high above Malabar Hill,
watching the whole island. In the afternoon's
sun-stunned silence a coconut fell.
A dog, his skin vibrating over bones
to rid him of flies, barked. And I fell ill:

kidney haemorrhage that oozed blood
into the bladder. I felt the hawk's beak
pull at a kidney, like a worm out of mud,
as my skin shrank and tightened over the weak
skeleton. All the pains the heart withstood,

and did not fall. A kind woman by my bed
kept vigil, telling a favourite tale:
how Babur, the Mogul King, prayed and tried
to bring back his son to life and grew pale
himself with Humayun's illness and died.

But Humayun had lived to rule. She said
a whole kingdom waited to see me crowned,
with the oil of life to anoint my head.
My body took shape like the chart, I found
the outline of bones fill with flesh and blood.

III

A crow shifted from his nest to a branch,
pulled his black tongue at the sun and let fall
a splotch of white into the shade. A finch
flew out. The crow laughed. An eagle, appalled,
moved to another tree. A snake looked, flinched.

India was at civil war,
the crow excreted where he pleased. And I,
reborn from a fairy-tale, saw bones charred
in mounds on pavements. It was no country
for princes, and the eagle soared

above the darker clouds. The undergrowth
heaved uneasily with poison of snakes.
'The heart is free!' people cried. 'What if truth
runs out like blood? We have our independence.'
The blood of India ran out with my youth.

The Town Clerk's Views

'Yes, the Town Clerk will see you.' In I went.
He was, like all Town Clerks, from north of Trent;
A man with bye-laws busy in his head
Whose Mayor and Council followed where he led.
His most capacious brain will make us cower,
His only weakness is a lust for power –
And that is not a weakness, people think,
When unaccompanied by bribes or drink.
So let us hear this cool careerist tell
His plans to turn our country into hell.
'I cannot say how shock'd I am to see
The *variations* in our scenery.
Just take for instance, at a casual glance,
Our muddled coastline opposite to France:
Dickensian houses by the Channel tides
With old hipp'd roofs and weather-boarded sides.
I blush to think one corner of our isle
Lacks concrete villas in the modern style.
Straight lines of hops in pale brown earth of Kent,
Yeomen's square houses once, no doubt, content
With willow-bordered horse-pond, oast-house, shed,
Wide orchard, garden walls of browny-red –
All useless now, but what fine sites they'ld be
For workers' flats and some light industry.
Those lumpy church towers, unadorned with spires,
And wavy roofs that burn like smouldering fires
In sharp spring sunlight over ashen flint
Are out of date as some old aquatint.
Then glance below the line of Sussex downs
To stucco terraces of seaside towns
Turn'd into flats and residential clubs
Above the wind-slashed Corporation shrubs.
Such Georgian relics should by now, I feel,
Be all rebuilt in glass and polished steel.

Bournemouth is looking up. I'm glad to say
That modernistic there has come to stay.
I walk the asphalt paths of Branksome Chine
In resin-scented air like strong Greek wine
And dream of cliffs of flats along those heights,
Floodlit at night with green electric lights.
But as for Dorset's flint and Purbeck stone,
Its old thatched farms in dips of down alone –
It should be merged with Hants and made to be
A self-contained and plann'd community.
Like Flint and Rutland, it is much too small
And has no reason to exist at all.
Of Devon one can hardly say the same,
But "South-West Area One" 's a better name
For those red sandstone cliffs that stain the sea
By mid-Victoria's Italy – Torquay.
And "South-West Area Two" could well include
The whole of Cornwall from Land's End to Bude.
Need I retrace my steps through other shires?
Pinnacled Somerset? Northampton's spires?
Burford's broad High Street is descending still
Stone-roofed and golden-walled her elmy hill
To meet the river Windrush. What a shame
Her houses are not brick and all the same.
Oxford is growing up to date at last.
Cambridge, I fear, is living in the past.
She needs more factories, not useless things
Like that great chapel which they keep at King's.
As for remote East Anglia, he who searches
Finds only thatch and vast, redundant churches.
But that's the dark side. I can safely say
A beauteous England's really on the way.
Already our hotels are pretty good
For those who're fond of *very simple food* –
Cod and two veg., free pepper, salt and mustard,
Followed by nice hard plums and lumpy custard,
A pint of bitter beer for one-and-four,
Then coffee in the lounge a shilling more.
In a few years this country will be looking

As uniform and tasty as its cooking.
Hamlets which fail to pass the planners' test
Will be demolished. We'll rebuild the rest
To look like Welwyn mixed with Middle West.
All fields we'll turn to sports grounds, lit at night
From concrete standards by fluorescent light:
And over all the land, instead of trees,
Clean poles and wire will whisper in the breeze.
We'll keep one ancient village just to show
What England once was when the times were slow –
Broadway for me. But here I know I must
Ask the opinion of our National Trust.
And ev'ry old cathedral that you enter
By then will be an Area Culture Centre.
Instead of nonsense about Death and Heaven
Lectures on civic duty will be given;
Eurhythmic classes dancing round the spire,
And economics courses in the choir.
So don't encourage tourists. Stay your hand
Until we've really got the country plann'd.'

The Interrogation

We could have crossed the road but hesitated.
And then came the patrol;
The leader conscientious and intent,
The men surly, indifferent.
While we stood by and waited
The interrogation began. He says the whole
Must come out now, who, what we are,
Where we have come from, with what purpose, whose
Country or camp we plot for or betray.
Question on question.
We have stood and answered through the standing day
And watched across the road beyond the hedge
The careless lovers in pairs go by,
Hand linked in hand, wandering another star,
So near we could shout to them. We cannot choose
Answer or action here,
Though still the careless lovers saunter by
And the thoughtless field is near.
We are on the very edge,
Endurance almost done,
And still the interrogation is going on.

Touch and Go

Man is coming out of the mountains
But his tail is caught in the pass.
Why does he not free himself
Is he not an ass?

Do not be impatient with him
He is bowed with passion and fret
He is not out of the mountains
He is not half out yet.

Look at his sorrowful eyes
His torn cheeks, his brow
He lies with his head in the dust
Is there no one to help him now?

No, there is no one to help him
Let him get on with it
Cry the ancient enemies of man
As they cough and spit.

The enemies of man are like trees
They stand with the sun in their branches
Is there no one to help my creature
Where he languishes?

Ah, the delicate creature
He lies with his head in the rubble
Pray that the moment pass
And the trouble.

Look he moves, that is more than a prayer,
But he is so slow
Will he come out of the mountains?
It is touch and go.

From Cathkin Braes: A View of Korea

This is a quiet ridge.
The stars come out, and the city
In its streetshine and smoke below me
Vibrating composes the dying
Day to order and calm.

On broken far-off Bloody
Ridge history stiffens
Slowly among the stained snows.
The ice creeps from yesterday
Into a stony truce.
The glittering craters are fixed,
Taut, sheeted, blank
Like shell-blinded earth-
Tears only thaw can shed
And roll down ravaged lines
In spring, upon the dead.
Can history make more
Of all that is held in this cold
Than: hordes who sleep in elegy?
Than: a night of flares and blood,
Shadows, the shriek of jets
And men like shadows running
From thicket to stunted thicket
Gaining a tree, an ambush,
An outpost, a shelter, a bullet,
Or down in some crawling convoy
Spattered by the blasting rocket-
Shots' disintegers, or lumbering
Wounded in doomed ambulance
To the rut that roofs a mine,
Or with white frostbitten hands
Gripping a truck-side, a flamethrower,
A rifle, a letter, or shoulders

Of a friend at the threshold of death,
Or worst this side of the atom
To be caught in the awful napalm
And wrapped in that inquisition
And blanket of secular fire
To scream unheeded to the stars
What man now hardly hears,
Since man has hardened man,
Contemning order and calm.

'This place was Bloody Ridge,
This place was Heartbreak Hill.'
As for the men, and the land,
They lie in the order of valour,
And desolation is its calm.

Choosing a Name

My little son, I have cast you out
  To hang heels upward, wailing over a world
  With walls too wide.
My faith till now, and now my love:
  No walls too wide for that to fill, no depth
  Too great for all you hide.

I love, not knowing what I love,
  I give, though ignorant for whom
  The history and power of a name.
I conjure with it, like a novice
  Summoning unknown spirits: answering me
  You take the word, and tame it.

Even as the gift of life
  You take the famous name you did not choose
  And make it new.
You and the name exchange a power:
  Its history is changed, becoming yours,
  And yours by this: who calls this, calls you.

Strong vessel of peace, and plenty promised,
  Into whose unsounded depths I pour
  This alien power;
Frail vessel, launched with a shawl for sail,
  Whose guiding spirit keeps his needle-quivering
  Poise between trust and terror,

And stares amazed to find himself alive;
  This is the means by which you say *I am*,
  Not to be lost till all is lost,
When at the sight of God you say *I am nothing*,
  And find, forgetting name and speech at last,
  A home not mine, dear outcast.

The Planners

Some who fell in love with lack of order
And liked the random weather, were made angry,
Accused the planners thus 'It is not brick
Only you set upright and scaffolding
And the roof bending at a perfect angle,
But all our love you end in measurements,
Construct a mood for any moment, teach
Passion to move in inches not by chance.'

And swarming from the forests to new houses
They chipped the walls a little, left footmarks
Across the thresholds, would not scan each other
By clock or compass, terrified the silence
With rough words that had never been thought out.

And builders, poets fell upon them, saw
A just disorder for their alteration,
Would turn the conversation into music,
Tidy the house and from the lovers' quarrel
Shape a whole scene with middle, end, beginning,
Never be wearied of the straightening out
Though would not recognise they fell in love
Most deeply at the centre of disaster.

Death of a Son

(who died in a mental hospital aged one)

Something has ceased to come along with me.
Something like a person: something very like one.
    And there was no nobility in it
      Or anything like that.

Something was there like a one year
Old house, dumb as stone. While the near buildings
    Sang like birds and laughed
      Understanding the pact

They were to have with silence. But he
Neither sang nor laughed. He did not bless silence
    Like bread, with words.
      He did not forsake silence.

But rather, like a house in mourning
Kept the eye turned in to watch the silence while
    The other houses like birds
      Sang around him.

And the breathing silence neither
Moved nor was still.

I have seen stones: I have seen brick
But this house was made up of neither bricks nor stone
    But a house of flesh and blood
      With flesh of stone

And bricks for blood. A house
Of stones and blood in breathing silence with the other
    Birds singing crazy on its chimneys.
      But this was silence,

This was something else, this was
Hearing and speaking though he was a house drawn
    Into silence, this was
        Something religious in his silence,

Something shining in his quiet,
This was different this was altogether something else:
    Though he never spoke, this
        Was something to do with death.

And then slowly the eye stopped looking
Inward. The silence rose and became still.
The look turned to the outer place and stopped,
    With the birds still shrilling around him.
        And as if he could speak

He turned over on his side with his one year
Red as a wound
He turned over as if he could be sorry for this
And out of his eyes two great tears rolled, like stones,
    And he died.

On an Afternoon Train
from Purley to Victoria, 1955

Hello, she said and startled me,
Nice day. Nice day I agreed.
I am a Quaker she said and Sunday
I was moved in silence
to speak a poem loudly
for racial brotherhood.

I was thoughtful, then said
what poem came on like that?
One the moment inspired she said.
I was again thoughtful.

Inexplicably I saw
empty city streets lit dimly
in a day's first hours.
Alongside in darkness
was my father's big banana field.

Where are you from? she said.
Jamaica I said.
What part of Africa is Jamaica? she said.
Where Ireland is near Lapland I said.
Hard to see why you leave
such sunny country she said.
Snow falls elsewhere I said.

So sincere she was beautiful
as people sat down around us.

November, 1956

It were best to sleep
Elections will proceed without our aid.

Jakov has lost the old encounter
Of naked flesh with steel
He hangs, feet in the air
Cold from a Danube lamp post

Where are the cigarettes? I inhale
The taste of railway stations

All night waits, remembering
The greasy faces at the hot-dog stands.

Mahmoud should know you cannot breathe
Face downward in the sand
We are policemen for his pyramids
Illiterates have no traffic on canals.

Somewhere in neverland, the telepeople
Broadcast and count and cheer
The general who will keep them out of war
Protect their interest and provide them beer.

Best to sleep, allowing these
Events their passage, while the dawn
Creeps in on London like a white disease.

Pleasure Drive

Children play on the by-pass, with the peaks
Of gasometers haunting them, and factories
Like lingering shapes of the past. Beyond, in fields,
Are massive artificial animals
And haystacks like Tibetan hats – the strange
Art of the simple. Lanes lead to villages
Selling beer and petrol as stores to mad explorers:
Behind the walls are superstitious rites,
Performed under pious mottoes worked in wool.

And so to higher land whose fortifications
Date back to fathers with somewhat smaller brains.
The roads and churches in the valley sink
Beneath old vegetation: further still
The opposing line of downs is menacing
As a rival system.

                Now we descend, the wind
Fresher, tinctured with chemicals, through
Light industries, across the estuary's bridge.
The point of this provincial city is
A tower that kept the river from the sea,
Particular from general. Like a rotten tooth,
Its walls disguise an empty centre where
Hundreds of birds festoon the greyish air,
Their droppings falling through the rooms of state
To pile up in the dungeons. In the squares
Of battlements fit sections of the city:
The railway's claws, the suburbs spread like fans,
And in a moat of green the similar
Cathedral stone, a different kind of ruin.

Time has irregularities, its grain
Leaves knots where the unfortunate remain,
Hacking against irrational designs.

Let us return to that metropolis
Whose fuming lights the sky, whose galleries
Blaze with ingenious art, whose sewers flow,
Where those in love are glad and soldiers only
Polish euphoniums and horses' rumps;
And not despise its anachronistic pleasures.
Even when classes do not slay each other
And generations accept their heritage,
In times of monolithic calm, the single
Life must enjoy its happiness between
Atrocious thoughts: the smiling driver who
Forever nears that unwished destination
Where his road ends in blood and wrecked machine.

After the Release of Ezra Pound

In Jerusalem I asked
the ancient Hebrew poets to forgive you,
and what would Walt Whitman have said
and Thomas Jefferson?

        Paul Potts

In Soho's square mile of unoriginal sin
where the fraudulent neon lights haunt,
but cannot hide, the dinginess of vice,
the jeans and sweater boys spoke of Pound,
and you, Paul, repeated your question.

The chi-chi bums in Torino's laughed and
the virgins of St Martin's School of Art.
The corner spivs with their Maltese masks
loitered for the two o'clock result,
and those in the restaurants of Greek Street,
eating income tax, did not hear the laugh.

Gentle Gentile, you asked the question.
Free now (and we praise this) Pound could answer.

The strip lighting of Soho did not fuse,
no blood trickled from a certain book
down the immaculate shelves of Zwemmer's.
But the circumcised did not laugh.
The swart nudes in the backrooms put on clothes
and the doors of the French pub closed.

Pound did not hear the raw Jewish cry,
the populations committed to the dark
when he muttered through microphones
of murderers. He, not I, must answer.

Because of the structures of a beautiful poet
you ask the man who is less than beautiful,
and wait in the public neurosis of Soho,
in the liberty of loneliness for an answer.

In the beer and espresso bars they talked
of Ezra Pound, excusing the silences of an old man,
saying there is so little time between
the parquet floors of an institution
and the boredom of the final box.

Why, Paul, if that ticking distance between
was merely a journey long enough
to walk the circumference of a Belsen,
Walt Whitman would have been eloquent,
and Thomas Jefferson would have cursed.

The Guardians

The young, having risen early, had gone,
Some with excursions beyond the bay-mouth,
Some toward lakes, a fragile reflected sun.
Thunder-heads drift, awkwardly, from the south;

The old watch them. They have watched the safe
Packed harbours topple under sudden gales,
Great tides irrupt, yachts burn at the wharf
That on clean seas pitched their effective sails.

There are silences. These, too, they endure:
Soft comings-on; soft after-shocks of calm.
Quietly they wade the disturbed shore;
Gather the dead as the first dead scrape home.

Changing the Subject

I had suggested, in exasperation, that he find
    something other to write about
Than the moon, the flowers, and birds, and temples,
    and the bare hills of the once holy city –

People, I proposed, who bravely push their way
    through the leprous lakes of mud.
It was the wet season, rain upon spittle and urine,
    and I had been bravely pushing my way.

It happened my hard words chimed with a new slogan,
    a good idea, since ruined –
'Humanism'. So I helped on a fashion, another like
    mambo, French chanson, and learning Russian.

Now he comes back, my poet, in a different guise:
    the singer of those who sleep in the subway.
'Welcome you are,' his vagrants declaim to each other,
    'a comrade of the common fate.'

'Are they miners from Kyushu?' he asks, these 'hobos
    all in rags.' And adds that
'Broken bamboo baskets, their constant companions, watch
    loyally over their sleeping masters.'

Thus my friend. He asks me if he has passed the test,
    is he truly humanistic,
Will I write another article, about his change of heart?
    I try to think of the subway sleepers.

Who are indescribable. Have no wives or daughters to sell.
    Not the grain of faith that makes a beggar.
Have no words. No thing to express. No 'comrade'.
    Nothing so gratifying as a 'common fate'.

Their broken bamboo baskets are loyal because no one
would wish to seduce them.
Their ochre skin still burns in its black nest, though a
hundred changed poets decide to sing them.

'Are they miners from Kyushu?' Neither he nor I will
ever dare to ask them.
For we know they are not really human, are as apt themes
for verse as the moon and the bare hills.

Innocent's Song

Who's that knocking on the window,
Who's that standing at the door,
What are all those presents
Lying on the kitchen floor?

Who is the smiling stranger
With hair as white as gin,
What is he doing with the children
And who could have let him in?

Why has he rubies on his fingers,
A cold, cold crown on his head,
Why, when he caws his carol,
Does the salty snow run red?

Why does he ferry my fireside
As a spider on a thread,
His fingers made of fuses
And his tongue of gingerbread?

Why does the world before him
Melt in a million suns,
Why do his yellow, yearning eyes
Burn like saffron buns?

Watch where he comes walking
Out of the Christmas flame,
Dancing, double-talking:

Herod is his name.

Lady Lazarus

I have done it again.
One year in every ten
I manage it –

A sort of walking miracle, my skin
Bright as a Nazi lampshade,
My right foot

A paperweight,
My face a featureless, fine
Jew linen.

Peel off the napkin
O my enemy.
Do I terrify? –

The nose, the eye pits, the full set of teeth?
The sour breath
Will vanish in a day.

Soon, soon the flesh
The grave cave ate will be
At home on me

And I a smiling woman.
I am only thirty.
And like the cat I have nine times to die.

This is Number Three.
What a trash
To annihilate each decade.

What a million filaments.
The peanut-crunching crowd
Shoves in to see

Them unwrap me hand and foot –
The big strip tease.
Gentlemen, ladies

These are my hands
My knees.
I may be skin and bone,

Nevertheless, I am the same, identical woman.
The first time it happened I was ten.
It was an accident.

The second time I meant
To last it out and not come back at all.
I rocked shut

As a seashell.
They had to call and call
And pick the worms off me like sticky pearls.

Dying
Is an art, like everything else.
I do it exceptionally well.

I do it so it feels like hell.
I do it so it feels real.
I guess you could say I've a call.

It's easy enough to do it in a cell.
It's easy enough to do it and stay put.
It's the theatrical

Comeback in broad day
To the same place, the same face, the same brute
Amused shout:

'A miracle!'
That knocks me out.
There is a charge

For the eyeing of my scars, there is a charge
For the hearing of my heart –
It really goes.

And there is a charge, a very large charge
For a word or a touch
Or a bit of blood

Or a piece of my hair or my clothes.
So, so, Herr Doktor.
So, Herr Enemy.

I am your opus,
I am your valuable,
The pure gold baby

That melts to a shriek.
I turn and burn.
Do not think I underestimate your great concern.

Ash, ash –
You poke and stir.
Flesh, bone, there is nothing there –

A cake of soap,
A wedding ring,
A gold filling.

Herr God, Herr Lucifer
Beware
Beware.

Out of the ash
I rise with my red hair
And I eat men like air.

Five Ways to Kill a Man

There are many cumbersome ways to kill a man.
You can make him carry a plank of wood
to the top of a hill and nail him to it. To do this
properly you require a crowd of people
wearing sandals, a cock that crows, a cloak
to dissect, a sponge, some vinegar and one
man to hammer the nails home.

Or you can take a length steel,
shaped and chased in a traditional way,
and attempt to pierce the metal cage he wears.
But for this you need white horses,
English trees, men with bows and arrows,
at least two flags, a prince and a
castle to hold your banquet in.

Dispensing with nobility, you may, if the wind
allows, blow gas at him. But then you need
a mile of mud sliced through with ditches,
not to mention black boots, bomb craters,
more mud, a plague of rats, a dozen songs
and some round hats made of steel.
In an age of aeroplanes, you may fly
miles above your victim and dispose of him by
pressing one small switch. All you then
require is an ocean to separate you, two
systems of government, a nation's scientists,
several factories, a psychopath and
land that no one needs for several years.

These are, as I began, cumbersome ways
to kill a man. Simpler, direct, and much more neat
is to see that he is living somewhere in the middle
of the twentieth century, and leave him there.

Order Me a Transparent Coffin
and Dig My Crazy Grave

After the next war ... the sky
Heaves with contaminated rain.
End to end our bodies lie
Round the world and back again.

Now from their concrete suites below
Statesmen demurely emanate
And down the line of millions go
To see the people lie in state.

Nikita Ikes, Franco de Gaulles,
Officiate and dig the holes.
Mao tse-sheks, Macadenauers,
Toting artificial flowers.

As they pay tribute each one wishes
The rain was less like tears, less hot, less thick.
They mutter, wise as blind white fishes,
Occasionally they are sick.

But I drily grin from my perspex coffin
As they trudge till they melt into the wet,
And I say: 'Keep on walking, keep on walking,
You bastards, you've got a hell of a way to walk yet.'

Winston Churchill

On the morning of the funeral,
when the cranes were practising their salute,
the Myth woke up to his last responsibility.
He elbowed his way into his braces,
each shoulder some sort of clinched strategy,
and the trousers settled like theatre curtains
over the last generation of shiny shoes.

The responsibility lay around
our semi in the form of symbols
just a bit too big to manage:
the British Warm that gave me aircraft-carrier
shoulders; five inches of measly bath water;
and a rhetoric, which my father could turn on
for the small fee of being believed.

Orange Drums, Tyrone, 1966

The lambeg balloons at his belly, weighs
Him back on his haunches, lodging thunder
Grossly there between his chin and his knees.
He is raised up by what he buckles under.

Each arm extended by a seasoned rod,
He parades behind it. And though the drummers
Are granted passage through the nodding crowd,
It is the drums preside, like giant tumours.

To every cocked ear, expert in its greed,
His battered signature subscribes 'No Pope'.
The goatskin's sometimes plastered with his blood.
The air is pounding like a stethoscope.

Let Me Die a Youngman's Death

Let me die a youngman's death
not a clean and inbetween
the sheets holywater death
not a famous-last-words
peaceful out of breath death

When I'm 73
and in constant good tumour
may I be mown down at dawn
by a bright red sports car
on my way home
from an allnight party

Or when I'm 91
with silver hair
and sitting in a barber's chair
may rival gangsters
with hamfisted tommyguns burst in
and give me a short back and insides

Or when I'm 104
and banned from the Cavern
may my mistress
catching me in bed with her daughter
and fearing for her son
cut me up into little pieces
and throw away every piece but one

Let me die a youngman's death
not a free from sin tiptoe in
candle wax and waning death
not a curtains drawn by angels borne
'what a nice way to go' death

Elizabeth

(In the summer of 1968 thousands of people turned out at the small
stations along the route to see the train carrying the body of Robert
Kennedy from New York to Arlington Memorial Cemetery in
Washington. In Elizabeth, New Jersey, three people were pressed
forward on to the line by the crowd and killed by a train coming the
other way – I happened to be travelling up by the next train in this
direction and passed the bodies. One was of a black woman.)

Up from Philadelphia,
Kennedy on my mind,
Found you waiting in Elizabeth,
Lying there by the line.

Up from Philadelphia,
Wasn't going back,
Saw you, then saw your handbag
Forty yards on up the track.

Saw you under a blanket,
Black legs sticking through,
Thought a lot about Kennedy,
Thought a lot about you.

Years later,

Blood on the line, blood on the line,
Elizabeth,
No end, no end to anything,
Nor any end to death.

No public grief by television,
Weeping all over town,
Nobody locked the train up
That struck the mourners down.

Nobody came to see you,
You weren't lying in state.
They swept you into a siding
And said the trains would be late.

They left you there in the siding
Against an outhouse wall
And the democratic primaries,
Oh they weren't affected at all,

In no way,

Blood on the line, blood on the line,
Elizabeth,
No end, no end to anything,
Nor any end to death.

Sirhan shot down Kennedy,
A bullet in L.A.,
But the one that broke Elizabeth,
It was coming the other way,

Coming on out of nowhere,
Into nowhere sped,
Blind as time, my darling,
Blind nothing in its head.

Elizabeth, Oh Elizabeth,
I cry your name and place
But you can't see under a blanket,
You can't see anyone's face,

Crying

Blood on the line, blood on the line,
Elizabeth,
No end, no end to anything,
Nor any end to death.

Music of the Spheres

I

'music please' and the man at the telescope
looks and listens looks and listens and waits

this vulgar Beethoven is thrust
like a crude vase on the mind's mantelpiece
to interrupt the monotony of space

pastoral valleys in a calculating brain
green waters to catch a falling star

yet it is partly true,
the star falls away incredibly
and what the old German scratched on paper
was true
of the giant nebulae that rolled away
past him into his green and silent night

II

it's only the last centimetre
that makes music

Ptolemy's little golden wheels
will shine for ever, they are laid
and numbered in silk-lined boxes,
in their time
they were the movement of God's brain
smoothly timeless on their jewelled bearings

the spheres are broken and their music
is war
they do not keep time with each other
for time bends

it is vain to cloud the sky over
with coarse noise to cheat the silence
for the silence slips through
a ghost of thin dust

it's only the last centimetre
where there's space enough for music
and for me to walk about in it listening

III

if they do
catch creation in the act
if they do
reach an edge that is really an edge
and not just the edge of their minds
if they do
trace time and space into
a new multifoliate rose

if they do
I'd like to stand at the last centimetre
where the long elipses touch down

and listen
to the old music taking the strain of the new
and putting out notes like snowdrops
as if
there had been no crushing weight of winter

A Disaster

There came news of a word.
Crow saw it killing men. He ate well.
He saw it bulldozing
Whole cities to rubble. Again he ate well.
He saw its excreta poisoning seas.
He became watchful.
He saw its breath burning whole lands
To dusty char.
He flew clear and peered.

The word oozed its way, all mouth,
Earless, eyeless.
He saw it sucking the cities
Like the nipples of a sow
Drinking out all the people
Till there were none left,
All digested inside the word.

Ravenous, the word tried its great lips
On the earth's bulge, like a giant lamprey –
There it started to suck.

But its effort weakened.
It could digest nothing but people.
So there it shrank, wrinkling weaker,
Puddling
Like a collapsing mushroom.
Finally, a drying salty lake.
Its era was over.
All that remained of it a brittle desert
Dazzling with the bones of earth's people

Where Crow walked and mused.

Under the Stone

They sleep out the day in Grimsby, Goole, or Hull,
The sleep of Empire sherry and unspeakable liquors,
And clumsily beg at the Saturday cinema queues
From steady workers and their penny-pinching girlfriends,
The washed and sober, who only want to laugh or listen.

These men remind them of the back of their minds.
Splendid barbarians, they form tribes in the slums
Up certain dim streets, the tribes of second-hand,
In empty houses no one wants to buy,
Abandoned rooms the poor have given up.

No one wants to see them, in a grey dawn, walk down
The empty streets, an army of unkept appointments,
Broken promises, as drab as fog,
Like portents meaning bad harvests, unemployment,
Cavalry in the streets, and children shouting 'Bread! Bread!'

But they mean nothing, they live under the stone.
They are their own failures and our nightmares
Or longings for squalor, the bad meanings we are.
They like it like that. It makes them happy,
Walking the rubble fields where once houses were.

Wounds

Here are two pictures from my father's head –
I have kept them like secrets until now:
First, the Ulster Division at the Somme
Going over the top with 'Fuck the Pope!'
'No Surrender!': a boy about to die,
Screaming 'Give 'em one for the Shankill!'
'Wilder than Gurkhas' were my father's words
Of admiration and bewilderment.
Next comes the London-Scottish padre
Resettling kilts with his swagger-stick,
With a stylish backhand and a prayer.
Over a landscape of dead buttocks
My father followed him for fifty years.
At last, a belated casualty,
He said – lead traces flaring till they hurt –
'I am dying for King and Country, slowly.'
I touched his hand, his thin head I touched.

Now, with military honours of a kind,
With his badges, his medals like rainbows,
His spinning compass, I bury beside him
Three teenage soldiers, bellies full of
Bullets and Irish beer, their flies undone.
A packet of Woodbines I throw in,
A lucifer, the Sacred Heart of Jesus
Paralysed as heavy guns put out
The night-light in a nursery for ever;
Also a bus-conductor's uniform –
He collapsed beside his carpet-slippers
Without a murmur, shot through the head
By a shivering boy who wandered in
Before they could turn the television down
Or tidy away the supper dishes.
To the children, to a bewildered wife,
I think 'Sorry Missus' was what he said.

Dancers at the Moy

This Italian square
And circling plain
Black once with mares
And their stallions,
The flat Blackwater
Turning its stones

Over hour after hour
As their hooves shone
And lifted together
Under the black rain,
One or other Greek war
Now coloured the town

Blacker than ever before
With hungry stallions
And their hungry mares
Like hammocks of skin,
The flat Blackwater
Unable to contain

Itself as horses poured
Over acres of grain
In a black and gold river.
No band of Athenians
Arrived at the Moy fair
To buy for their campaign,

Peace having been declared
And a treaty signed.
The black and gold river
Ended as a trickle of brown
Where those horses tore
At briars and whins,

Ate the flesh of each other
Like people in famine.
The flat Blackwater
Hobbled on its stones
With a wild stagger
And sag in its backbone,

The local people gathered
Up the white skeletons.
Horses buried for years
Under the foundations
Give their earthen floors
The ease of trampolines.

High Windows

When I see a couple of kids
And guess he's fucking her and she's
Taking pills or wearing a diaphragm,
I know this is paradise

Everyone old has dreamed of all their lives –
Bonds and gestures pushed to one side
Like an outdated combine harvester,
And everyone young going down the long slide

To happiness, endlessly. I wonder if
Anyone looked at me, forty years back,
And thought, *That'll be the life;*
No God any more, or sweating in the dark

About hell and that, or having to hide
What you think of the priest. He
And his lot will all go down the long slide
Like free bloody birds. And immediately

Rather than words comes the thought of high windows:
The sun-comprehending glass,
And beyond it, the deep blue air, that shows
Nothing, and is nowhere, and is endless.

At the Castle Hotel, Taunton

Today it's not scones but tea-cakes
    (And the sound of ambulances
    in the reconstructed streets) –

Rich voices are discussing the new Warden
    (The Show is the best for years,
    the architects' watercolours outstanding) –

Pearls and brogues survive, cashmere clings
    (Is this the Ark of Adultery
    or two old friends killing time?) –

Interlopers must wait for their tea
    (There's only one waitress on today,
    her footsteps are masked on the stairs) –

Hands want something to do, eyes won't idle
    (*Country Life* in a rexine folder,
    who buys, who sells all these houses?) –

O impossible England under the modern stars
    (Mr Edward du Cann thanks the voters
    of Taunton for their generous support) –

So much beauty, so unexpectedly preserved
    (And we two strangers have today
    honoured gentle Eliot at East Coker) –

Not only the pheasant eating by the road
    (And the cider factory, the industrial
    archaeology with the rural) –

But the pattern of beauty changing in the air
    (Fields painted by history, a steam
    of seasons softening what lives) –

Somerset for survivors and a good thing too
 (*Seventeenth-century farmhouse,*
 part-converted, owner abroad) –

Seen from Ilminster spire, everything is safe
 (It is being kept for posterity
 but where do the people of England live?)

The Soho Hospital for Women

1

Strange room, from this angle:
white door open before me,
strange bed, mechanical hum, white lights.
There will be stranger rooms to come.

As I almost slept I saw the deep flower opening
and leaned over into it, gratefully.
It swimmingly closed in my face. I was not ready.
It was not death, it was acceptance.

*

Our thin patient cat died purring,
her small triangular head tilted back,
the nurse's fingers caressing her throat,
my hand on her shrunken spine; the quick needle.

That was the second death by cancer.
The first is not for me to speak of.
It was telephone calls and brave letters
and a friend's hand bleeding under the coffin.

*

Doctor, I am not afraid of a word.
But neither do I wish to embrace that visitor,
to engulf it as Hine-Nui-te-Po
engulfed Maui; that would be the way of it.

And she was the winner there: her womb crushed him.
Goddesses can do these things.
But I have admitted the gloved hands and the speculum
and must part my ordinary legs to the surgeon's knife.

2

Nellie has only one breast
ample enough to make several.
Her quilted dressing-gown softens
to semi-doubtful this imbalance
and there's no starched vanity
in our abundant ward-mother:
her silvery hair's in braids, her slippers
loll, her weathered smile holds true.
When she dresses up in her black
with her glittering marcasite brooch on
to go for the weekly radium treatment
she's the bright star of the taxi-party –
whatever may be growing under her ribs.

*

Doris hardly smokes in the ward –
and hardly eats more than a dreamy spoonful –
but the corridors and bathrooms
reek of her Players Number 10,
and the drug-trolley pauses
for long minutes by her bed.
Each week for the taxi-outing
she puts on her skirt again
and has to pin the slack waistband
more tightly over her scarlet sweater.
Her face, a white shadow through smoked glass,
lets Soho display itself unregarded.

*

Third in the car is Mrs Golding
who never smiles. And why should she?

3

The senior consultant on his rounds
murmurs in so subdued a voice
to the students marshalled behind
that they gather in, forming a cell,

a cluster, a rosette around him
as he stands at the foot of my bed
going through my notes with them,
half-audibly instructive, grave.

The slight ache as I strain forward
to listen still seems imagined.

Then he turns his practised smile on me:
'How are you this morning?' 'Fine,
very well, thank you.' I smile too.
And possibly all that murmurs within me
is the slow dissolving of stitches.

4

I am out in the supermarket choosing –
this very afternoon, this day –
picking up tomatoes, cheese, bread,

things I want and shall be using
to make myself a meal, while they
eat their stodgy suppers in bed:

Janet with her big freckled breasts,
her prim Scots voice, her one friend,
and never in hospital before,

who came in to have a few tests
and now can't see where they'll end;
and Coral in the bed by the door

who whimpered and gasped behind a screen
with nurses to and fro all night
and far too much of the day;

pallid, bewildered, nineteen.
And Mary, who will be all right
but gradually. And Alice, who may.

Whereas I stand almost intact,
giddy with freedom, not with pain.
I lift my light basket, observing

how little I needed in fact;
and move to the checkout, to the rain,
to the lights and the long street curving.

Flying to Belfast, 1977

It was possible to laugh
as the engines whistled to the boil,

and wonder what the clouds looked like –
shovelled snow, Apple Charlotte,

Tufty Tails ... I enjoyed
the Irish Sea, the ships were faults

in a dark expanse of linen.
And then Belfast below, a radio

with its back ripped off,
among the agricultural abstract

of the fields. Intricate,
neat and orderly. The windows

gleamed like drops of solder –
everything was wired up.

I thought of wedding presents,
white tea things

grouped on a dresser,
as we entered the cloud

and were nowhere –
a bride in a veil, laughing

at the sense of event, only
half afraid of an empty house

with its curtains boiling
from the bedroom window.

In a Notebook

There was a river overhung with trees
With wooden houses built along its shallows
From which the morning sun drew up a haze
And the gyrations of the early swallows
Paid no attention to the gentle breeze
Which spoke discreetly from the weeping willows.
There was a jetty by the forest clearing
Where a small boat was tugging at its mooring.

And night still lingered underneath the eaves.
In the dark houseboats families were stirring
And Chinese soup was cooked on charcoal stoves.
Then one by one there came into the clearing
Mothers and daughters bowed beneath their sheaves.
The silent children gathered round me staring
And the shy soldiers setting out for battle
Asked for a cigarette and laughed a little.

From low canoes old men laid out their nets
While on the bank young boys with lines were fishing.
The wicker traps were drawn up by their floats.
The girls stood waist-deep in the river washing
Or tossed the day's rice on enamel plates
And I sat drinking bitter coffee wishing
The tide would turn to bring me to my senses
After the pleasant war and the evasive answers.

There was a river overhung with trees.
The girls stood waist-deep in the river washing,
And night still lingered underneath the eaves
While on the bank young boys with lines were fishing.
Mothers and daughters bowed beneath their sheaves
While I sat drinking bitter coffee wishing –
And the tide turned and brought me to my senses.
The pleasant war brought the unpleasant answers.

The villages are burnt, the cities void;
The morning light has left the river view;
The distant followers have been dismayed;
And I'm afraid, reading this passage now,
That everything I knew has been destroyed
By those whom I admired but never knew;
The laughing soldiers fought to their defeat
And I'm afraid most of my friends are dead.

The Old Soap Opera

When Uncle Cecil fled to Europe
with his wicked baggage,
he left behind him,
cluttering the larder,
thirty tins of the golden syrup
he used to sign
into his porridge.
I went to stay with daunting aunts:
three sisters, who shared a wry,
yellow toothbrush,
and read the airmail from my father
in turn
through the plump and glaucous eye
of a magnifying-glass.
(I took this once,
to dazzle Mr Corcoran,
their gardener,
who chased me indoors with a handfork
that bristled with clods and worms.)
They spoke to each other of 'poor Cec'
and 'the devil's handiwork',
but found me an old yapp album,
where, in a blizzard of lace
and swaddled like Captain Scott,
he lay in his mother's arms;
or, naked in a summer hammock,
seemed not to notice the bumblebee
that lit on his forehead
like a benediction.
But there was something odd about the family
and, at his own wedding-reception,
he pretended to be a cuckoo-clock,
which worried Aunt Hester, his bride.
Later, he went swanning off to Biarritz

with a bathing beauty,
bear-hugged a girl in a garden
and dissipated his entire fortune
on prostitutes
in a blustery autumn
of banknotes, jewellery, loose change...
On one of his rare visits,
Mr Otterburn, the missionary preacher,
told me that 'the young lassies'
were 'queer fish', and I could see
how he peeled off and pocketed
his awkward wire glasses
in feminine company,
or stepped around
to the safe side of the furniture.
He had travelled
'all over Asia'
and nearly married a princess,
but 'she refused baptism'.
Mr Evans, who fell off a mountain
and now kerb-crawled through town
in a motorized Bath-chair,
took up gadgetry with naïve enthusiasm
and caught his wife and a brigadier
in a burglar-trap of his own invention.
Aunt Hester, I heard,
had plucked the brooch from her bosom
and chased a young girl through a London park,
lunging with the pin and shouting,
'You cow! You cow!'
And I can remember even now
the sweet perfume
of apples left to pucker in a dish
in somebody's dark
and unfrequented dining-room –
a smell I connect somehow
with Cousin Penny, 'snatched away'
by the richest man in Australia.
He kept a retinue

of gloomy servants, guard-dogs
and (his confidant and spy)
a raucous white cockatoo.
The marriage was a failure.

Line on the Grass

Shadow in the mind,
this is its territory:
a sweep of broken ground
between two guarded towns.

A tank engine rusting
in the long grass, a man
with a fly rod wading
in the grey river.

This looks so fixed, it could
be anytime; but, scanned
in the daylight, the fields
of crops, their hawthorn hedges,

seem too visible. The men
riding black bikes stiffly
along the road are passing
a burnt-out customs post

on an asphalt apron.
They are observed passing,
passing, in a dull light:
civilians at four o'clock.

Turned Out Nice Again

After der floodlights floodlighting der Kop
After the silence when the other's scored
After der referee's whistle saying stop
Sometimes yer just feel bloody bored.
The yard-dogs yelling and the winos chanting
Flinging of bog-rolls over distant terraces
He what was waving his rattle is now married
We what cheered Roger Hunt are getting on
And we don't bloody like it.

   Here there's no hollies but only werk
Werk an no hollies an der bloody cars
Like a traffic jam going out onto the tarmac
Which is a tarmac without footee, I can tell yer.
If there were hollies we'd fuck off ter Spain
   If there were footee
   An no werk
   If there were werk
   An you didn't have to do none
   If there were footee
   A five a side
   A kick round in der compound
   With no under-the-arm foreman bastard ter snitch on yer
But there is no footee.

   Who's dat der other side of yous?
I feel so pissed I can't add up to three
Only waitin there for de 14c

There's this other feller dressed up like a hippie
It mightn't be a feller for all I know
Anyhow, bollocks, who the fuck is it?

   What is dat noise?
It sounds to me like me old mam snivvelling
Who are them divvies runnin over building sites

In der nuttins
Streaking and kung-fuing each other
And falling arse-over-tip?
What are them flats
Blown to buggery wid leaky gas mains:
John F. Kennedy Heights, Everton Heights,
Belem Towers,
Nuttin.

In this beat-up hole, flat as a run-over cat,
In trainees and denims the yobs is singing
About the libree with the smashed-in winders.
There is an empty libree cos the staff's gone home
It's got no winders now an the door's kicked in;
We hate buiks.
Only Froggo stud up in r tree house
We took yous! We took yous!
Then it hissed down.

Der Mersey'd gone out an der sky caved in
We was like drowned rats, honest
An all the owl dossers with them bus passes just sat tight

YERARLRITE S See yer next match
I'd touch yer up but yer'd get me wrong
Me Da brought us up manly but you're me mates
YERARLRITE I'm not sharing no cell
With no old headerballs
Yer better off on yer own honest
Only sometimes when yer wake up in the night on yer tod
Sometimes yer dreamed of a busted Bessy Braddock

I sat on a bench in Anfield Cemetery
Should I keep on wid der Christmas Club dyer reckon?
Higsons Brewery's gone on strike, gone on strike, gone on strike
r Mavis at the Witches House on New Brighton Prom
We love you Keegan oh yes we do
Make date for homo action
Scotty from Speke is ace is last

I write this so I can lay der classy berds
D'yer want a knuckle butty? That soft boy's here again.
Poor owl everyone.

YERARLRITE YERARLRITE YERARLRITE

England at Christmas, *1982*

O silly little, proud and silly, country
so good at ceremonial, limited wars,
football (occasionally)! Snob Billy Buntery
gives all the rich, rich presents – Santa Claus
has handed out the land. He hates the serfs,
the common people, so uncommonly low;
loves dogs, cats, hunting, cricket, the green turfs
that make a stately-homely postcard show –
quite beautiful, memorials to old greed,
when what there was to take, to steal, to pinch
went to the bastard Baron on his steed
or landowners, enclosing each square inch,

or City men, who raise a joyous anthem
for a fake-lady bossyboots from Grantham.

These Boys

These boys, fifteen, sixteen, seventeen, heeding
Not God nor social worker, being young the old therefore
Abjure. Her few pounds and her radio they care for

And steal, but do not care to leave her bleeding,
Nor break her flaky arms, nor black her eyes,
Nor crack with a brick her skull, though this is common.

Into her stair cupboard they scoop the little woman
Where, in her own damp and dark, at length she dies,
Of all deaths surely the most terrible.

What's to be done with such as these our children,
The untaught, the unfit, the unkind, the unnatural?
What right have we to pity or to pardon?

O bury them deep, deep in desolate places.
Stop eyes, ears, mouths with earth. My face is not these faces.
Each day somewhere the same, or worse disgraces.

Visitors: Armthorpe, August 1984

Four of them, sitting in the kitchen
drinking tea, I imagine saucers.
I am probably wrong about the saucers.
A hot August day in the kitchen.

'*The back door was unlocked*
but they kicked it in.
Police said "Send the bastards out"
then the policeman jammed the door

into my face'. I imagine a kitchen,
I am probably wrong about the saucers.
I imagine heartbroken saucers
with patterns of flowers.

'This is unclean'

This is unclean: to eat turbots on Tuesdays,
tying the turban unclockwise at cockcrow,
cutting the beard in a south-facing mirror,
wearing the mitre whilst sipping the Bovril,
chawing the pig and the hen and the ox-tail,
kissing of crosses with peckers erected,
pinching of bottoms (except in a yashmak),
flapping of cocks at the star-spangled-banner,
snatching the claret-pot off of the vicar,
munching the wafer without genuflexion,
facing the East with the arse pointing backwards,
thinking of something a little bit risqué,
raising the cassock to show off the Y-fronts,
holding a Homburg without proper licence,
chewing the cud with another man's cattle,
groping the ladies – or gentry – o'Sundays,
leaving the tip on the old-plum-tree-shaker,
speaking in physics instead of the Claptrap,
failing to pay due obeisance to monkeys,
loving the platypus more than the True Duck,
death without Afterlife, smirking in Mecca,
laughing at funny hats, holding the tenet
how that the Word be but fucking baloney,
failing to laud the Accipiter which Our Lord saith is Wisdom.

Started by *Australopithecus*, these are
time-honoured Creeds (and all unHoly doubters
shall be enlightened by Pious Devices:
mayhems of tinytots, low flying hardwares,
kneecappings, letterbombs, deaths of the firstborns,
total extinctions of infidel unclean wrong-godded others).

My Lover

For I will consider my lover, who shall remain nameless.

For at the age of 49 he can make the noise of five different kinds of
   lorry changing gear on a hill.

For he sometimes does this on the stairs at his place of work.

For he is embarrassed when people overhear him.

For he can also imitate at least three different kinds of train.

For these include the London tube train, the steam engine, and the
   Southern Rail electric.

For he supports Tottenham Hotspur with joyful and unswerving
   devotion.

For he abhors Arsenal, whose supporters are uncivilized and
   rough.

For he explains that Spurs are magic, whereas Arsenal are boring
   and defensive.

For I knew nothing of this six months ago, nor did I want to.

For now it all enchants me.

For this he performs in ten degrees.

For first he presents himself as a nice, serious, liberated person.

For secondly he sits through many lunches, discussing life and
   love and never mentioning football.

For thirdly he is careful not to reveal how much he dislikes losing
   an argument.

For fourthly he talks about the women in his past, acknowledging
   that some of it must have been his fault.

For fifthly he is so obviously reasonable that you are inclined to
   doubt this.

For sixthly he invites himself round for a drink one evening.

For seventhly you consume two bottles of wine between you.

For eighthly he stays the night.

For ninthly you cannot wait to see him again.

For tenthly he does not get in touch for several days.

For having achieved his object he turns again to his other interests.

For he will not miss his evening class or his choir practice for
   a woman.

For he is out nearly all the time.

For you cannot even get him on the telephone.

For he is the kind of man who has been driving women round the bend for generations.

For, sad to say, this thought does not bring you to your senses.

For he is charming.

For he is good with animals and children.

For his voice is both reassuring and sexy.

For he drives an A-registration Vauxhall Astra estate.

For he goes at 80 miles per hour on the motorways.

For when I plead with him he says, 'I'm not going any slower than *this*.'

For he is convinced he knows his way around better than anyone else on earth.

For he does not encourage suggestions from his passengers.

For if he ever got lost there would be hell to pay.

For he sometimes makes me sleep on the wrong side of my own bed.

For he cannot be bossed around.

For he has this grace, that he is happy to eat fish fingers or Chinese takeaway or to cook the supper himself.

For he knows about my cooking and is realistic.

For he makes me smooth cocoa with bubbles on the top.

For he drinks and smokes at least as much as I do.

For he is obsessed with sex.

For he would never say it is overrated.

For he grew up before the permissive society and remembers his adolescence.

For he does not insist it is healthy and natural, nor does he ask me what I would like him to do.

For he has a few ideas of his own.

For he has never been able to sleep much and talks with me late into the night.

For we wear each other out with our wakefulness.

For he makes me feel like a light-bulb that cannot switch itself off.

For he inspires poem after poem.

For he is clean and tidy but not too concerned with his appearance.

For he lets the barber cut his hair too short and goes round looking like a convict for a fortnight.

For when I ask if this necklace is all right he replies, 'Yes, if no
    means looking at three others.'
For he was shocked when younger team-mates began using
    talcum powder in the changing-room.
For his old-fashioned masculinity is the cause of continual
    merriment on my part.
For this puzzles him.

The Missing

Now as I watch the progress of the plague,
The friends surrounding me fall sick, grow thin,
And drop away. Bared, is my shape less vague
– Sharply exposed and with a sculpted skin?

I do not like the statue's chill contour,
Not nowadays. The warmth investing me
Led outward through mind, limb, feeling, and more
In an involved increasing family.

Contact of friend led to another friend,
Supple entwinement through the living mass
Which for all that I knew might have no end,
Image of an unlimited embrace.

I did not just feel ease, though comfortable:
Aggressive as in some ideal of sport,
With ceaseless movement thrilling through the whole,
Their push kept me as firm as their support.

But death – Their deaths have left me less defined:
It was their pulsing presence made me clear.
I borrowed from it, I was unconfined,
Who tonight balance unsupported here,

Eyes glaring from raw marble, in a pose
Languorously part-buried in the block,
Shins perfect and no calves, as if I froze
Between potential and a finished work.

– Abandoned incomplete, shape of a shape,
In which exact detail shows the more strange,
Trapped in unwholeness, I find no escape
Back to the play of constant give and change.

August 1987

Bus Talk

Of all the bloody cheek. How the hell would they feel
if they pulled their bathroom curtains back and found
the bottom of their garden slumped in the river
and their new greenhouse leaning over like a tent

with half the pegs pulled out? 'Don't worry Mr Argot,'
they said, 'your house is built on a plane of bedrock.'
Apparently it's the frost that's done this that and the other
to the soil. I said that might be very true

but the frost isn't going to put it back is it?
And the insurance won't pay. Sent a bloke round
with a spirit-level; couldn't have been here ten minutes
before he was up and off. I said listen, mate,

I used to be an engineer, I know subsidence
when I see it. He said it would have to look
like the Brighton bombing before they'd even think
of forking out. Don't you worry, pal, I said,

if you have to pull me out of the rubble
with my tackle hanging out and half the world there watching
I'll drag you through court so fast you won't know
if you're coming or going. I mean,

I don't know why he bothered coming round:
he didn't know goose shit from tapioca.
Only this morning the alarm clock had walked
to the edge of the drawers. It would have smashed

to smithereens but it went off and I woke up
and caught it. And I can't put eggs down anywhere.
No, if that house hasn't dropped a good two inches
this last eighteen months, my cock's a kipper.

Translating the English, 1989

'... and much of the poetry, alas, is lost in translation...'

Welcome to my country! We have here Edwina Currie
and The Sun newspaper. Much excitement.
Also the weather has been most improving
even in February. Daffodils. (Wordsworth. Up North.) If you like
Shakespeare or even Opera we have too the Black Market.
For two hundred quids we are talking Les Miserables,
nods being as good as winks. Don't eat the eggs.
Wheel-clamp. Dogs. Vagrants. A tour of our wonderful
capital city is not to be missed. The Fergie,
The Princess Di and the football hooligan, truly you will
like it here, Squire. Also we can be talking crack, smack
and Carling Black Label if we are so inclined. Don't
drink the H_2O. All very proud we now have
a green Prime Minister. What colour yours? Binbags.
You will be knowing of Charles Dickens and Terry Wogan
and Scotland. All this can be arranged for cash no questions.
Ireland not on. Fish and chips and the Official Secrets Act
second to none. Here we go. We are liking
a smashing good time like estate agents and Neighbours,
also Brookside for we are allowed four Channels.
How many you have? Last night of Proms. Andrew
Lloyd-Webber. Jeffrey Archer. Plenty culture you will be agreeing.
Also history and buildings. The Houses of Lords. Docklands.
Many thrills and high interest rates for own good. Muggers.
Much lead in petrol. Filth. Rule Britannia and child abuse.
Electronic tagging, Boss, ten pints and plenty rape. Queen Mum.
Channel Tunnel. You get here fast no problem to my country
my country my country welcome welcome welcome.

Death to Poll Tax

The doctor expects your mother to die
sometime during the night.

I am trying to get out at Piccadilly Circus
A man says sorry the exits are all closed.
Go back down. Leicester Square, the same thing happens.
I start to make the noise the tube makes
coming into the station. I imagine a fabulous
fire, licking its long lips through the tunnels
crossing the blue line into the red line into the black.

The first thing, at Tottenham Court Road, is a long line of masked
    men.
The second thing: a jagged star made from space
where the window was; two Hitachi TVs face down
on the street. The third thing is a man screaming
DEATH TO POLL TAX – a policeman punching him every time
he gets to Poll. Death to Poll THUD Tax. His voice is going
like the sirens in the distance.

The fourth thing: a man running, a child in each hand.
Come on Come on Come on. Hurry up.
I rush through the back streets. I have no map.
When I do arrive at the Cous Cous House
Kathryn is there: red lipstick, black silk top, neat bob.
I apologise for being late. We eat falafel.

You are in my kitchen waiting. What time I ask?
Eight o'clock you say. Sooner than they thought.

Initial Illumination

Farne cormorants with catches in their beaks
shower fishscale confetti on the shining sea.
The first bright weather here for many weeks
for my Sunday G-Day train bound for Dundee,
off to St Andrew's to record a reading,
doubtful, in these dark days, what poems can do,
and watching the mists round Lindisfarne receding
my doubt extends to Dark Age Good Book too.
Eadfrith the Saxon scribe/illuminator
incorporated cormorants I'm seeing fly
round the same island thirteen centuries later
into the *In principio*'s initial I.
Billfrith's begemmed and jewelled boards got looted
by raiders gung-ho for booty and berserk,
the sort of soldiery that's still recruited
to do today's dictators' dirty work,
but the initials in St John and in St Mark
graced with local cormorants in ages,
we of a darker still keep calling Dark,
survive in those illuminated pages.
The word of God so beautifully scripted
by Eadfrith and Billfrith the anchorite
Pentagon conners have once again conscripted
to gloss the cross on the precision sight.
Candlepower, steady hand, gold leaf, a brush
were all that Eadfrith had to beautify
the word of God much bandied by George Bush
whose word illuminated midnight sky
and confused the Baghdad cock who was betrayed
by bombs into believing day was dawning
and crowed his heart out at the deadly raid
and didn't live to greet the proper morning.

Now with noonday headlights in Kuwait
and the burial of the blackened in Baghdad
let them remember, all those who celebrate,
that their good news is someone else's bad
or the light will never dawn on poor Mankind.
Is it open-armed at all that victory V,
that insular initial intertwined
with slack-necked cormorants from black laquered sea,
with trumpets bulled and bellicose and blowing
for what men claim as victories in their wars,
with the fire-hailing cock and all those crowing
who don't yet smell the dunghill at their claws?

Video Tale of a Patriot

for David Maxwell

START. Eton. Hice. Beaten
    in some grim urban/hopeless northern
seat. Afforded southern chances.
    Rosette. Recount. Speech. Dances.
Member. Lobbies. Froth. Committees.
    Old wife. New wife. Boards. City's.
Sir. Riches. Burgundy. Soak.
    Lord. Bypass. Bypass. Croak.

Sorry, REWIND: bypass-bypass-
    lord-soak-burgundy-riches-
sir. PLAY. 'Sir: I am increasingly
concerned at the let's say increasingly
unpredictable, unclassifiable,
    unconstructive, unreliable,
incomprehensible, reprehensible,
    a-moral, im-moral, not very sensible

acts of citizens of England of late.
    Acts not actually threatening the State
but thoroughly disconcerting. Sir:
    I saw a her who was kissing a her.
I heard the young call enemies brothers.
    I felt my money being spent on others
lying in slums, doing nothing for it.
    I smelt filth. Though I try to ignore it

it won't go away. I see vague vicars
    plastering cars with political stickers.
I read about princes visiting thieves,
    and a lord who cares what a lout believes.

I took down the numbers of those I saw
    shouting *We don't want this no more*
outside the school where a shocking percent
    appeared to have no idea what I meant,

or even what it means to be born
    a Briton. I tell you, a day will dawn
when everyone does what the blazes he wants,
    bangs his drums and performs his sundance
on what was once a proud green land,
    ruled with a disciplining spotless hand
correctly. Sir, a gent, I am sure, would
    agree with me when I –' STOP. FAST FORWARD.

The Scale of Intensity

1) Not felt. Smoke still rises vertically. In sensitive individuals, déjà vu, mild amnesia. Sea like a mirror.

2) Detected by persons at rest or favourably placed, i.e. in upper floors, hammocks, cathedrals etc. Leaves rustle.

3) Light sleepers wake. Glasses chink. Hairpins, paperclips display slight magnetic properties. Irritability. Vibration like passing of light trucks.

4) Small bells ring. Small increase in surface tension and viscosity of certain liquids. Domestic violence. Furniture overturned.

5) Heavy sleepers wake. Public demonstrations. Large flags fly. Vibration like passing of heavy trucks.

6) Large bells ring. Bookburning. Aurora visible in daylight hours. Unprovoked assaults on strangers. Glassware broken. Loose tiles fly from roof.

7) Weak chimneys broken off at roofline. Waves on small ponds, water turbid with mud. Unprovoked assaults on neighbours. Large static charges built up on windows, mirrors, television screens.

8) Perceptible increase in weight of stationary objects: books, cups, pens heavy to lift. Fall of stucco and some masonry. Systematic rape of women and young girls. Sand craters. Cracks in wet ground.

9) Small trees uprooted. Bathwater drains in reverse vortex. Wholesale slaughter of religious and ethnic minorities. Conspicuous cracks in ground. Damage to reservoirs and underground pipelines.

10) Large trees uprooted. Measurable tide in puddles, teacups, etc. Torture and rape of small children. Irreparable damage to foundations. Rails bend. Sand shifts horizontally on beaches.

11) Standing impossible. Widespread self-mutilation. Corposant visible on pylons, lampposts, metal railings. Most bridges destroyed.

12) Damage total. Movement of hour hand perceptible. Large rock masses displaced. Sea white.

Postsoviet Postmodern

Vaike–Oismae, Tallinn

Launched by the Soviet Sixties, this scheme
for a suburb in concentric rings says moon-base,
says orbiting station: a hand-me-down dream
    from American sci-fi. Remember the Space Race?
    Cosmonauts on launchpads in the Khazakh
    dust, pot-roasted secretly at the state's
discretion? Now we wake to stains and cracks,
the creep of concrete cancer much the same
as relicts of the Sixties anywhere: Caracas,
    Wandsworth. But vineberry swarms up to claim
    ten storey cliffs, each creeper a ripped seam
    of autumn. Each block wears a shirt of flame.

The Pumping Station's down again; half
Tallinn's hot taps gurgle dry. I'm in an eighth
floor flat, bussed to a cousin's for a bath.
    On TV, a Mexican dream of L.A.: ghost-
    Spanish moves the lips. Curt as an epitaph,
    Estonian subtitles. Russian, dubbed almost
in synch. Slipped through cracks in the scene
a stray *porque?* like a weed in a pavement. My host
has left *Women's Day: Australia's Biggest Magazine*
    (from other cousins) where I'll see. '*Aussie Man Relates*
    Penis Mutilation' '*Diana – Sexpot Or Ice Queen?*'
    with a Japanese remote control for paperweight.

Outside, there's scrub encroaching. Waste ground.
A cow at a stake. A dirt track. And a frontier
with what's gone. That low grassed-over mound
    should be a long barrow, but the door
    is dented steel – a reinforced surround,
    a man-sized catflap. Now we're echoes in a corridor,
an air-raid-shelter hush one step could detonate,

but lined with lock-ups, dozens, like a bullion store.
Ours rattles up, bumping its counterweight,
    a cylinder block, and there's the family car,
    the great grey Lada like a warrior in state
    among shelves racked with gravegoods, jar on jar
of gherkin flesh crammed into murky green.
Lab specimens. And garnet glints: a ruined bar
of bottles – vodka, 'Churchill's London Gin' –
    transfused with redcurrant juice, like every year
    in every farm's earth-cellar till the history machine
    crashed from the sky and left us stranded here.

Neighbours

When the rains come in Rwanda in a Tutsi village
and the topsoil's washed away, strange shoots
of fingers, toes, knees and elbows, jawbones,

push up from such wrong, unlikely roots
as have lain there since they were slaughtered –
the cowherd and the teacher and the sawbones

and their women and their children and their neighbours
(for unless you are a hermit in a mountain cavern
or a guru in a temple in the jungle, neighbours

are what you naturally, inevitably have,
to share your sunsets and the fruits of your labours),
all waiting quietly now for when they are watered,

when the rains come, in Rwanda, in a Tutsi village.

Millennium Bug

'The bug threatens a domino-effect global collapse of computer systems
at midnight on 31 December 1999. Designed in the sixties with a two-digit
number representing the day, month and year, computers are unable to
recognise a change of century which requires four digits. Thus at the
turn of the year 2000, the new century will be 00, which computers will
understand as 1900. And the fear is it could lead to a Mad Max-type
Armageddon.'   David Atkinson, *The Big Issue*, 20–26 May 1996

What do they expect when they heed not
   the dance of numbers?

Blunders and bloomers
   will be their undoing

bugs will flower in their computers
   for it is written a day will come

when the angel of mayhem
   appears in their IT systems

and demons disguised as digits
   trumpet the collapse of world markets

that trespass on the human soul
   and treat people as dispensable

and the millennium will toll
   its software Armageddon

and zero will be lifted high
   as the laughter of Galileo

and Pythagoras too will erupt
   at the mention of bankrupt

and the Devil alone
   shall sing in praise

of the counting frame
   and runic rods
   and notched bone

Mythology

Earth's axle creaks; the year jolts on; the trees
begin to slip their brittle leaves, their flakes of rust;
and darkness takes the edge of daylight, not
because it wants to – never that. Because it must.

And you? Your life was not your own to keep
or lose. Beside the river, swerving under ground,
your future tracked you, snapping at your heels:
Diana, breathless, hunted by your own quick hounds.

Mother Scrubbing the Floor

She had a dancer's feet, elegant, witty.
We had our father's, maverick spreaders of dirt.

Dirt from London, dirt from Kent
Mud, dust, grass, droppings, wetness, *things*,
Dirt barefaced, dirt stinking, dirt invisible.

Whatever it was, she was ready:
The rubber kneeler, clanking galvanised bucket,
The Lifebuoy, the hard hot water.

Let me! we'd say, meaning *Hate to see you do this.*
Too old. Too resentful. Besides, you'll blame us
That you had to do it.

She never yielded. We couldn't do it right,
Lacking her hatred of filth, her fine strong hands.

Don't want you to do this, she said. *Don't want you to have to.*
Just remember this: love isn't sex
But the dreary things you do for the people you love.
And 'Home is the girl's prison,
The woman's workhouse.' Not me; Shaw.

I do remember. I stand where she knelt.

Poem for the End of the World

Some day, it seems, the cosmos,
Turning impatient, will throw a planet at us,
Or else a filthy snowball of a comet,
Or we will stifle in our effluent.
That sort of thing, we're told
Put paid to the dinosaurs –
Lumbering Diplodocus, leggy Iguanodon,
Baroque Triceratops and Stegasaur –
Our childhood friends, or the earth's childhood.
And that will be the ultimate news from nowhere –
For us and our computers.

Some find it reassuring to suppose
An elvish folk will land –
Grass-green men from outer space,
Or from the hollow centre of the earth, –
In delicate porcelain flying saucers –
Peter Pan or Noddy at their head.
Lob-lie-by-the-fire will tidy up our muddle -
It is his métier.

After *Götterdämmerung*, the Nordic myth recounted,
Baldr returns and his companions –
Beautiful gods who died and were forgotten.
Then in the scorched grass, they'll find the golden chessmen
That they had played with once
Before the first creation of the world.

NOTES AND ACKNOWLEDGEMENTS

NOTES

1900 THOMAS HARDY *The Darkling Thrush* The Victorians regarded 31 December 1900 as the end of the nineteenth century, though there was little to celebrate, as the country was embroiled in the frustrating and increasingly costly Boer War. Hardy's natural pessimism was deepened by the mounting death toll, with its 'hourly posted sheets of scheduled slaughter', as he put it in another poem. The war lasted till 1902.

1901 GEORGE MEREDITH *At the Funeral* The old queen went out with the old century. Meredith, one of the surviving literary giants of her reign, produced an elegy untypical only in its succinctness.

1902 FRANCES CORNFORD *Autumn Morning at Cambridge* Frances Cornford was in her teens when she wrote this buoyant and forward-looking poem, which catches the excitement and possibility of a new century 'sweeping up the leaves to let the people pass'. The battles ahead for women's suffrage and equality in education would put quite a wind up the men's gowns.

1903 JOHN MASEFIELD *Cargoes* A deceptively simple poem with an impressive range, both historical and geographical. Somehow Masefield manages to invest the dirty British coaster with all the romance of its predecessors on the old trade routes, and, by extension, give a heroic colouring to the mundane trade on which Britain's greatness rested. Masefield had joined the Merchant Navy at thirteen, and came to public notice with his *Salt Water Ballads* (1902).

1904 G. K. MENZIES *Frames of Mind Punch* still played an important part in national life, and printed much topical verse of variable quality. Income tax had been unpopular since its first introduction (in 1799) to pay for the Napoleonic wars. It had been abolished and then reintroduced, and despite Gladstone's pledge to remove it, it remained a fact of life, rising in the twentieth century to pay for increased social welfare. (In 1904 James Joyce showed what he thought of redistributive public finance, refusing to pay an income demand of three shillings and sixpence.)

1905 FRANCIS THOMPSON *At Lord's* Surprisingly, perhaps, the tortured author of 'The Hound of Heaven', was also a keen cricket follower, and in his last years would occasionally be persuaded to Lord's, though the experience tended to provoke nostalgia for the game's Golden Age when he regularly attended Old Trafford. The match described is the first encounter between Gloucestershire and Lancashire in 1878. The game was drawn.

'O my Hornby and my Barlow': the Lancashire opening batsmen. 'The champion of the centuries': W. G. Grace, the first to score 100 first-class hundreds. 'The long-whiskered Doctor': his elder brother, E.M. 'G.F.': W.G.'s younger brother. All three played for England.

1906 WALTER DE LA MARE *The Massacre* Echoes of Browning's 'Childe Roland to the Dark Tower Came' and Lewis Carroll's 'Jabberwocky' ('The vorpal blade went snicker-snack!').

1907 RUDYARD KIPLING *The Sons of Martha* 'As long as breath remains, he will remain the poet of the Empire', as one contemporary commentary had it. While wholeheartedly endorsing, and to a degree, shaping Britain's imperial ideology, Kipling never forgot or patronized the humble cohorts on which it relied. Soldiers, engineers, nurses, even the disgraced gentlemen rankers in India – all were beneficiaries of his imaginative sympathy and technical mastery.

Mary and Martha: Luke X, 38–42. Jesus was welcomed into the house of two sisters. Mary sat at his feet 'and heard his word', while Martha prepared and served the meal. When she protested, 'Jesus answered and said unto her, Martha, thou art careful and troubled about many things; / But one thing is needful: and Mary hath chosen that good part, which shall not be taken away from her.'

1908 W. H. DAVIES *A Beggar's Life* W. H. Davies, who continued a life of inspired vagrancy even after losing a foot jumping a train in Canada, was clearly a son of Mary rather than Martha.

1909 JOHN DAVIDSON *Song for the Twenty-fourth of March* Empire Day, instituted in 1902 by Edward VII to commemorate Queen Victoria's birthday. Davidson deploys his considerable metrical skill in the service of the fervent jingoism that fuelled the arms-race with Germany in the build-up to the First World War. Popular sentiment was particularly outraged at the Kaiser's attempt to match the British navy. Britain developed the new invincible Dreadnought, and undertook a rapid building programme, cheered on by such slogans as 'We want eight, and we won't wait'. Each ship cost £2 million. Davidson's imperial enthusiasm did not protect him from depression, and he drowned himself off the Cornish coast later in the year.

1910 JAMES ELROY FLECKER *Ballad of Camden Town* Virginia Woolf declared that 'human nature changed ... in or about 1910'. Certainly the new century saw the breaking up of the polar ice-cap of Victorian sexual mores as this and the next poem attest.

1911 ANNA WICKHAM *Divorce* Anna Wickham was born in Australia, which may account for her confident independence of spirit. Marriage to an amateur astronomer proved deadening and nearly deadly. 'Divorce' comes from her first (privately printed) volume, in response to which, rather than letting her go, her husband had her committed to a lunatic asylum.

1912 KATHLEEN EMERSON *'Oh! who are these in scant array?* From *Holloway Jingles*, a pamphlet of poems written by suffragettes incarcerated as a result of direct action to further their cause. Police brutality and the forced feeding of those on hunger strikes were features of an increasingly vicious deadlock.

1913 G. K. CHESTERTON *A Song of Swords* Like the suffragette agitation, Ireland was another burning political problem. Although the Prime Minister Asquith was at last in a position to push through the Liberal dream of Home Rule, mounting resistance in Ulster threatened civil war, and by 1914, after a conference with the leaders of the Nationalists and the Loyalists, Asquith wrote of 'an impasse with unspeakable consequences, upon a matter which to English eyes seems inconceivably small and to Irish eyes immeasurably big ... a real tragedy.' Although the onset of war brought about an uneasy truce, the tragedy burst out again in the Easter Rising of 1916, and subsequently throughout the rest of the century.

'The place called Swords' is a few miles outside Dublin and has a monastery founded by St Columba.

1914   RUPERT BROOKE *1914: Peace* It has been estimated that one and a half million poems were written in August, the vast majority hailing the war with varying degrees of delight. Rupert Brooke's series of sonnets (including 'The Soldier': 'If I should die, think only this of me...') undoubtedly caught the public mood. Brooke died, a national hero, virtually canonised, the following year, so never saw the hideous irony the Western Front made of his 'swimmers into cleanness leaping'.

Older, wiser men like John Masefield sounded a more cautious note, reflecting on past wars and those who were called upon to suffer

> the misery of the soaking trench,
> The freezing in the rigging, the despair
> In the revolting second of the wrench
> When the blind soul is flung upon the air,
>
> And died (uncouthly, most) in foreign lands
> For some idea but dimly understood
> Of an English city never built by hands
> Which love of England prompted and made good.

1915   EDWARD THOMAS *'This is No Case of Petty Right or Wrong'* Thomas articulates a similar instinctive patriotism, while distancing himself from the war hysteria generated by the papers. Across Europe, many took the view that the war itself 'was a consequence of the impoverishment of the imagination brought about by the mass press' (Niall Ferguson, *The Pity of War*). Thomas joined up in 1915 and was killed two years later.

1916   A. P. HERBERT *'The General inspecting the trenches'* The battle of the Somme – 1 July to the end of November – produced scarcely credible casualties (60,000 on the first day alone) for barely measurable gains, and gave rise to the perception of the British soldiers as 'lions led by donkeys'. Shute, seen in the front line more regularly than most top brass, was by no means a bad general, but his strict army ways made him unpopular when he took command of the Royal Naval Division. He was unlucky that the fledgling humorist A. P. Herbert was one of his junior officers. This piece of scatological protest was adopted as a marching song not just by the Naval Division but throughout the whole army. I have taken it from Lyn MacDonald's volume, *Somme*.

1917   SIEGFRIED SASSOON *The Effect* War-weariness, cynicism, and a slow-burning anger had set in by 1917, the year sections of the French army mutinied. Sassoon was by no means a lone dissident voice, but as a decorated serving officer and widely-read poet, he posed an embarrassing challenge to the authorities. His loathing of the 'yellow-pressmen' was intense. The role of the papers in prolonging the carnage was generally acknowledged, Lloyd George, the Prime Minister, admitting (December 1917) 'If the people really knew ... the war would be stopped tomorrow'. For Hitler, trying to explain – and learn from – Germany's defeat, the Northcliffe press propaganda seemed 'an inspired work of genius'. (Quotes from Ferguson, *The Pity of War*.)

1918   WILFRED OWEN *Spring Offensive* The last of Owen's war poems, and
arguably the most powerful, not least for its poignant juxtaposition of the
beauty of the natural world and the almost certain destruction of those
involved in any offensive action. Even when the stalemate of trench
warfare was broken down in the last months of the war, casualties
remained horrifyingly high. Owen himself died a week before the
Armistice in a fierce action to cross the Sambre Canal in which two
Victoria Crosses were won.

　'[All their strange day]': cancelled in the manuscript, but as Owen's
editor Jon Stallworthy makes clear, 'WO intended to find alternatives'.
Most editions print the full line.

1919   EZRA POUND from *Hugh Selwyn Mauberley* Pound's harsh view of the
war became the accepted one in the Twenties as the cost of the 'war to end
war' was gradually digested. Nearly ten million combatants were killed
and, including the wounded, the total casualty figure was nearly 33 million.
Casualties for the British Empire topped 3 million. Britain also spent in the
region of 45 billion dollars on the war, so there was precious little money
to build the promised 'homes fit for heroes'. (Figures from Ferguson, *The
Pity of War*.)

1920   W. B. YEATS *The Second Coming* Often assumed to have been a pointer to
the apocalypse of the Second World War, Yeats's most famous short poem
was in fact written out of the despair engendered by the first. He published
it (twice) in 1920 before collecting it in *Michael Robartes and the Dancer*
(1921).

　'*Spiritus Mundi*': Yeats's 'warehouse of supersensual Platonic forms'
(John Unterecker).

1921   CHARLOTTE MEW *Saturday Market* Although the war gave a huge boost
to social change, and in particular forced greater freedom for women after
their important work in munitions factories etc, the pace of change in rural
areas was slow. Although her output was slight, Mew attracted serious
notice with her first book, *The Farmer's Bride*, and Thomas Hardy called
her 'far and away the best living woman poet'. She had a close affinity with
the vulnerable and distressed, and committed suicide herself in 1928.

1922   A. E. HOUSMAN *Eight O'Clock* A. E. Housman was the acknowledged
master of small-town misery and anonymous rural tragedy, and the lyric
fatalism of *A Shropshire Lad* had made it highly popular during the war.
Housman wrote little and published less, so a new collection
(characteristically titled *Last Poems*) was a major literary event of the year.
(Others were the US publication of 'The Waste Land', after its first
appearance in *The Criterion* – and the Paris publication of *Ulysses*.)

1923   HILAIRE BELLOC *Ballade of Genuine Concern* Secure in his catholicism
and bumptious self-confidence, Belloc delighted, rather than despaired, at
human folly. Here he fabricates a fantasy crisis from the underlying
volatility (and makes witty use of the ballade's usually rather plodding
Envoi).

1924   IVOR GURNEY *Old Tale* Like so many veterans of the war, Ivor Gurney
never fully recovered from his experiences on the Western Front. A
natural lyricist like John Clare, Gurney also ended his days in a lunatic
asylum, where he continued to write both poetry and music.

1925   T. S. ELIOT *The Hollow Men* Born of the personal crisis that would lead
Eliot to join the Church of England, this is also a representative expression
of Twenties aridity and ennui.

1926   IDRIS DAVIES *'Do you remember 1926?'* Davies, one of the most politically
committed poets of the inter-war years, wrote *The Angry Summer*, a
lengthy sequence of poems about the miners' strike which triggered the
General Strike, in 1926. The bitterness is perhaps better distilled in this
section from his *Gwalia Deserta* (1938).

1927   HAROLD MONRO *Midnight Lamentation* Monro played an influential role
as founder of the Poetry Bookshop and publisher of many of the century's
new voices. His own poetry was dispassionately pessimistic.

1928   EDGELL RICKWORD *Luxury* In the Twenties, Rickword indulged in a
near-Swiftian disgust at both the dutiful role-play of suburban domesticity
and the self-deluding and corrupt society at large, before committing
himself to overtly left-wing political satire in the thirties. He was an early
disciple of Eliot, 'the poet who has most effectively upheld the reality of the
art in an age of preposterous poeticising' (1925) – (though viciously
dismissive of his conversion to orthodox religion) – and has perhaps been
unjustly neglected.

1929   D. H. LAWRENCE *Change of Government* Nettles rather than Pansies as
Lawrence reacts to the election in which Ramsay MacDonald entered 10
Downing Street (for the second time) as Prime Minister of a minority
Labour government against a background of wild scaremongering about
the Red menace. He was in fact no more radical than Tony Blair. In the
same year Lawrence's paintings were confiscated as obscene and the
stockmarket on Wall Street collapsed.

1930   ROBERT GRAVES *Song: Lift-Boy* As the Jazz Age gave way to the
Depression, Graves captures the almost jaunty sense of despair.
'Old Eagle': possible reference to US emblem on dollar bills.

1931   BASIL BUNTING *Aus Dem Zweiten Reich* Reportage on the last days of the
Weimar Republic. Bunting was in Germany only 'for a very short time, for
I found I didn't like the Germans at all'. Instead, he 'went to Rapallo and
settled down there close to Pound'. Of the prolific playwright in the third
section, he noted: 'The great man need not be identified but will ... be
recognized by those who knew him' (later confirmed by Bunting as the
ageing novelist, poet and playwright Gerhart Hauptmann, 1862–1946).
'fabelhaft': marvellous. 'Shrecklich': dreadful.

1932   STEPHEN SPENDER *The Express* In developing, with Auden and C. Day
Lewis, a new aesthetic of the modern industrial landscape, Spender
provided the press the excuse to coin the handy title The Pylon Poets.

1933   NAOMI MITCHISON *The Midsummer Apple Tree* A bold poem for a woman
to publish (in *Time and Tide*) in 1933, but representative of the new sexual
freedoms to be found, particularly in left-wing circles.

1934   W. H. AUDEN *A Bride in the 30's* The defining voice of the Thirties.
Auden's analysis of Europe's crisis was grounded equally in Freud and
Marx, enabling him to bridge brilliantly the gap between the public and
private spheres. He later felt he had compromised his poetic integrity in

some of his more overtly political poems like 'Spain' (1937), which he dropped from the canon. 'A Bride in the 30's' survived, though with light revision and two stanzas (12 and 13) cut. These are restored here in the original version taken from *The English Auden* (ed. Edward Mendelson).

Van der Lubbe: Dutch communist executed for the Reichstag fire of 1932, which provided the Nazis with a convenient propaganda platform against the Left.

1935 HUGH MACDIARMID *After Two Thousand Years* The dominant Scottish poet of the century, Hugh MacDiarmid (pseudonym of Christopher Murray Grieve) wore his socialist sympathies on his sleeve, and famously expressed his contempt for the English political poets of the Thirties: 'You cannot light a match on a crumbling wall.'

1936 JOHN CORNFORD *A Letter from Aragon* Cornford was one of the politically committed young men who joined the International Brigade to fight for Spain's elected government against Franco's fascist uprising. He was killed in action on, or the day after, his twenty-first birthday (27 December 1936).

1937 WILLIAM EMPSON *Missing Dates* Though he satirized poets on the left for their determined pessimism – 'Waiting for the end, boys, waiting for the end' ('Just a Smack at Auden') – Empson was not immune to the general sense of gloom. Whatever its personal occasion, 'Missing Dates' captures the Thirties malaise perfectly, without a single topical reference. According to Empson's own Note: 'It is true about the old dog, at least I saw it reported somewhere, but the legend that a fifth or some such part of the soil of China is given up to ancestral tombs is (by the way) not true.'

1938 LOUIS MACNEICE from *Autumn Journal* Section VII of MacNeice's masterpiece conveys the universal if jittery and guilty relief at Neville Chamberlain's successful appeasement of Hitler at Munich. At the cost of much loss of face and the Czech Sudetenland, war was averted, but most suspected that the Prime Minister's emergence on the steps of the plane, proclaiming 'Peace in our time' and fluttering his bit of paper with Hitler's signature on it, merely put the country under starter's orders.

'Uebermensch' (Übermensch): superman.

1939 EDMUND BLUNDEN *A Window in Germany* A veteran of the Western Front, Blunden was one of those incapable of contemplating another war with Germany, and who did everything possible, by cultural exchanges and personal embassies, to promote mutual understanding between the two countries. (Another was the former England cricket captain C. B. Fry, who took it upon himself to explain to the Führer in person the difference between the Boy Scouts and the Hitler Youth.) As the date of this poem indicates, Blunden maintained a belief in the possibility of peace right up to the last minute. War was declared on 3 September after Germany ignored the British ultimatum to withdraw its troops from Poland.

1940 HENRY REED *Naming of Parts* (from *Lessons of the War*) There was little or no rejoicing at the outbreak of hostilities as there had been in 1914. Henry Reed's classic poem of basic training captures the mood of the average recruit, as does Alun Lewis's 'All day it has rained':

... we talked of girls and dropping bombs on Rome,

And thought of the quiet dead and the loud celebrities
Exhorting us to slaughter, and the herded refugees;
– Yet thought softly, morosely of them, and as indifferently
As of ourselves or those whom we
For years have loved, and will again
Tomorrow maybe love; but now it is the rain
Possesses us entirely, the twilight and the rain.

1941 DYLAN THOMAS *Among Those Killed in the Dawn Raid was a Man Aged a Hundred* From the onset of the Blitz the previous year, civilian casualties of the Luftwaffe's bombers were recorded almost daily. Dylan Thomas was working on a BBC project when he read this news item (about a raid on Hull), and wrote a draft of the poem then and there.

1942 ALAN ROSS *Survivors* Isolated after the fall of France, the country depended for its survival on the Royal Air Force (Battle of Britain, July–October 1940) and the Royal Navy and Merchant Navy, whose convoys broke the German seige. Alan Ross was in the Navy and was himself a survivor of a ship sunk by U-boat action on the arctic route to Russia.

1943 KEITH DOUGLAS *Sportsmen* Douglas served in North Africa, taking part in the Alamein campaign in 1942 (see his prose account, *From Alamein to Zem-Zem*). Like the First World War, the Second accelerated social change, further tilting the balance of power away from the so-called ruling classes – a development confirmed by the election victory of Attlee's Labour Party in 1945. Douglas registers the shift with his usual cool detachment. (Compare also Evelyn Waugh, *Brideshead Revisited*).
'I think I am becoming a God': deathbed joke of Vespasian, Roman Emperor AD 69–79 (he was in fact deified after his death). 'an 88': see next poem.

1944 GEOFFREY HOLLOWAY *Rhine Jump, 1944* After the Normandy landings (D-Day, 6 June 1944), the allied armies met fierce resistance from the retreating German forces. Parachute drops were one way of keeping up the momentum of the advance, though clearly fraught with danger for those taking part.

1945 PHILLIP WHITFIELD *Day of Liberation, Bergen-Belsen, May 1945* Rumours of the Nazis' Final Solution had been widespread for some time, and the Russians had already uncovered the horrors of Auschwitz (January 1945), but Belsen was still an appalling shock to the British soldiers who liberated it. A pile of naked female corpses, 80 yards long by 30 yards wide and four feet high, was just one of the sights that met them. Whitfield was a Captain in the Royal Army Medical Corps.
May saw the end of the war in Europe, and, after the two atomic bombs dropped on Hiroshima and Nagasaki in August, the Japanese also surrendered.

1946 R. S. THOMAS *The Village* After six years of conflict costing some 55 million lives worldwide, the ordinariness of peace became inestimably valuable.

1947 ZULFIKAR GHOSE *The Body's Independence* Not that the end of the war brought an end of global conflict. When India was granted independence and hastily partitioned by the new Labour government, there was a massive death toll as Hindus and Muslims fled to and from the newly created Pakistan. Ghose was born in Sialkot in 1935 and moved to England in 1959, taking a degree from Keele, and becoming cricket correspondent for the *Observer*.

1948　JOHN BETJEMAN　*The Town Clerk's Views* Always sharply opinionated about what was worth preserving and what was not ('Come, friendly bombs, and fall on Slough / It isn't fit for humans now', he wrote in 1937), Betjeman assumed the role of ardent defender of Britain's architectural heritage after the war. This satirical fantasy proved more prophetic than could have been guessed at the time.

1949　EDWIN MUIR　*The Interrogation* After the war, Muir was stationed by the British Council in Prague. There, he and his wife, Willa (with whom he translated Kafka) 'saw the iron curtain fall and ... their friends gradually finding it safer to avoid their company' (T. S. Eliot).

1950　STEVIE SMITH　*Touch and Go* Stevie Smith makes no overt reference to current events, but global tension was high due to the continuing Cold War in Europe, and the outbreak of hostilities when the communist North invaded South Korea.

1951　EDWIN MORGAN　*From Cathkin Braes: A View of Korea* Supported by British and Commonwealth troops, the United States committed themselves to 'the war we can't win, we can't lose, we can't quit' – though it was of considerably shorter duration than their entanglement in Vietnam.

　　　Bloody Ridge and Heartbreak Hill: 'the Hills of Korea: the cratered and shell torn, rat and lice infested peaks which the Americans called "real estate" ... Hills had to be clawed up by painful inches in the face of lashing fire and hails of hand grenades; to be captured and held; to be endlessly and back-breakingly dug and wired ... to be shelled off, overrun and re-taken; to be buried alive on or to die on – hills with names like Pork Chop Hill, the Punch Bowl, Frostbite Ridge, Old Baldy, Bloody Ridge and the Brown Bastard; hills which became "home" for the soldiers who fought for them' (Tim Carew, *The Korean War*, 1970).

1952　ANNE RIDLER　*Choosing a Name* For most, however, the Fifties offered a period of domestic retrenchment after the upheavals of the previous decades. Anne Ridler was writing and publishing in the Thirties and has continued producing accomplished poems on personal themes, both secular and overtly Christian, ever since.

1953　ELIZABETH JENNINGS　*The Planners* Another overtly Christian poet, Jennings has somehow seemed less comfortable with self, faith and society. She is widely admired for the honesty with which she has addressed her unease.

1954　JON SILKIN　*Death of a Son* A poem both of its time and as timeless as Ben Jonson's 'On My First Son' ('Rest in soft peace, and, ask'd, say here doth lye / Ben. Jonson his best piece of poetrie').

1955　JAMES BERRY　*On an Afternoon Train from Purley to Victoria, 1955* 1955 saw the first large-scale immigration from the Caribbean. James Berry, settled from Jamaica since 1948, was able to chart the West Indian experience from the beginning, often using a persona – Lucy in his case – to convey the immigrant's viewpoint. This device has also been employed by Grace

Nichols (in her Fat Black Woman poems), E. A. Markham (Lambchops) and Fred D'Aguiar (Mamma Dot), who have continued the tradition of black writing in a predominantly white and frequently racist culture along with, among others, Linton Kwesi Johnson, Benjamin Zephaniah, Jean 'Binta' Breeze, David Dabydeen, John Agard and Lemn Sissay.

1956   EVAN JONES *November, 1956* Evan Jones, another Jamaican, who came to England in 1956, the year in which the Soviet Union invaded Hungary and Britain and France embarrassed themselves by invading Egypt in an attempt to secure the Suez Canal. The election referred to was the American presidential election in which Eisenhower was re-elected.

1957   ROY FULLER *Pleasure Drive* The Prime Minister Harold Macmillan famously announced that 'most of our people have never had it so good'. Driving on uncrowded roads was one of the bonuses of life in the Fifties. (The first section of the M1 was opened in November 1959.)

1958   DANNIE ABSE *After the Release of Ezra Pound* Lucky to escape execution as a traitor for his active support of the Mussolini regime during the Second World War (on grounds of insanity), Pound was incarcerated in St Elizabeth's Hospital, Washington, DC, for twelve years, until pressure from such figures as T. S. Eliot and Robert Frost resulted in his release and repatriation to Italy. Once back on Italian soil he declared: 'The Fascist dictators made a mistake in the way they persecuted the Jews. The mistake was not in fighting the Jews, but the manner in which the Jews were fought. Rather than attack them as a bloc, each case should have been examined individually.' He also posed for photographers with his arm raised in a Fascist salute. (Humphrey Carpenter, *A Serious Character: The Life of Ezra Pound*)

1959   GEOFFREY HILL *The Guardians* Hill's first collection, *For the Unfallen*, introduced a new and powerful voice, undoubtedly of, but clearly out of sympathy with, the second half of the century.

1960   D. J. ENRIGHT *Changing the Subject* Enright is one of many British poets to have taught in, and written about, Japan. Others include Empson, Blunden, Anthony Thwaite and James Kirkup.

1961   CHARLES CAUSLEY *Innocent's Song* Causley is reminiscent of de la Mare in weaving the dark magic of fairy tale and myth into seemingly simple poems.

1962   SYLVIA PLATH *Lady Lazarus* October 1962 was the most productive month of Plath's life, with poems that made her second collection, *Ariel* (1965), such an extraordinary *tour de force* coming virtually every day – twenty-five in all.

1963   EDWIN BROCK *Five Ways to Kill a Man* Though life was undoubtedly more comfortable, it was, paradoxically, perceived to be under far greater threat than ever before, with almost instantaneous nuclear annihilation hanging over vast, well-provided-for populations. The Cuban Missile crisis of the previous year was just the latest in a series of near-misses.

1964   ADRIAN MITCHELL *Order me a Transparent Coffin and Dig My Crazy Grave* Adrian Mitchell was one of those in sympathy with the peace movement of the late Fifties and Sixties – the Campaign for Nuclear

Disarmament (CND) was launched in 1958 – and is best known perhaps for his protest poems 'Tell Me Lies About Vietnam' and '15 Million Plastic Bags'. 'Order me a Transparent Coffin' is driven by the same burning concern to save the world from the madness of those in authority.

Stanza 3 conflates the names of world leaders: Nikita Kruschev (USSR) and Dwight D. Eisenhower ('Ike') (US); Bahamonde Franco (Spain) and Charles de Gaulle (France); Mao tse Tung (Communist China) and Chiang Kai-shek (Nationalist China); Harold Macmillan (Great Britain) and Konrad Adenaur (West Germany)

1965 DAVID SCOTT *Winston Churchill* The towering British leader of the century, a truly patriarchal figure, whose state funeral was memorably transmitted to the nation in patchy black-and-white television images.

1966 SEAMUS HEANEY *Orange Drums, Tyrone, 1966* Heightened sectarian tension in Northern Ireland provoked by Protestant assertiveness. Ian Paisley refounded the Ulster Protestant Volunteers.

1967 ROGER MCGOUGH *Let Me Die A Youngman's Death* The best-selling *Mersey Scene* brought McGough, Adrian Henri and Brian Patten to prominence as poet-successors to the Beatles.

1968 KIT WRIGHT *Elizabeth* For the Americans, the Sixties 'began with idealism and hope for positive change, [but] ended with cynicism about government, distrust of politicians, violence and suspicion that dark conspiracies were at work behind closed doors in Washington' (Gavin Esler, *The United States of Anger*). J. F. Kennedy had been shot in Dallas in 1963. The assassination of his younger brother, Bobby, in the run-up to the Presidential election followed hard on the heels of Martin Luther King's murder, throwing America into a state of turmoil.

1969 ROBIN FULTON *Music of the Spheres* Despite their domestic troubles, the Americans still continued with the things they were best at, beating the Russians to land the first men on the moon (21 July). Apart from Auden's brilliant if rather dismissive 'Moon Landing' – 'It's natural the Boys should whoop it up for / so huge a phallic triumph, an adventure / it would not have occurred to women / to think worth while ...' – there seem to have been few contemporary poems on the subject. In this one Robin Fulton meditates on the ramifications of space exploration.

1970 TED HUGHES *A Disaster* (from *Crow*) Hughes had been a dominant voice since the publication of *A Hawk in the Rain* (1957), but *Crow* ('From the Life and Songs of the Crow') made an even more clamorous claim for attention, coining global despair from the pain of personal tragedy. It has sharply divided critics, but as John Carey said after Hughes's death, *Crow* 'is likely to prove his most powerful and original work' (*Sunday Times*, 1 November 1998)

'There came news of a word ...': compare John I, 1: 'In the beginning was the Word...'

1971 DOUGLAS DUNN *Under the Stone* From his first book, *Terry Street* (1969), set in the slums of Hull, Dunn has been a keen, if not unduly sentimental, student of inner-city lowlife.

1972 MICHAEL LONGLEY *Wounds* A feature of the latest round of 'Troubles' in Northern Ireland has been the squalid sectarian murder, a subject also tackled with great power by Seamus Heaney (see particularly section VII of 'Station Island'). 'Wounds' also indicates how long a shadow the First World War cast, especially the first morning of the battle of the Somme, when thousands of Irish volunteers were massacred by German machine-gun fire.

1973 PAUL MULDOON *Dancers at the Moy* Another star of Northern Ireland's post-war poetry renaissance, Paul Muldoon has proved prodigiously talented and prolific, exhibiting from the start 'a lively storyteller's wit combined with a crypticism that fascinates rather than defeats the reader' (Bernard O'Donoghue). He published his first collection, *New Weather*, at twenty-two, and has been effecting subtle but far-reaching climate changes in poetry written in English ever since.

1974 PHILIP LARKIN *High Windows* Widely popular and hugely influential, Philip Larkin's standing depended on a very modest output. With volumes coming out at ten-yearly intervals, each was a keenly anticipated event. The last, *High Windows*, was no exception. Like the more famous 'Annus Mirabilis' ('Sexual intercourse began / In nineteen sixty-three...'), though with a rare hint of transcendence, the title poem reflects on the huge shift in sexual mores that had taken place during Larkin's lifetime.

1975 PETER PORTER *At the Castle Hotel, Taunton* A lightly mocking view of his adoptive country's complacent heartlands by this prolific Australian-born poet, described by Philip Hobsbaum as 'not only a satirist but a rhetorician'.
Mr Edward du Cann: high-profile and influential Conservative MP for Taunton 1956–87.

1976 FLEUR ADCOCK *The Soho Hospital for Women* Cancer has a claim to be the disease of the century. For a contrasting approach, see Peter Reading's *C*.
'Hine-Nui-te-Po / engulfed Maui': 'Hine-Nui-te-Po was the Maori goddess of death. Maui, the trickster figure in Polynesian mythology, decided to kill her while she was asleep by crawling up into her vagina and out through her mouth, but she woke up and clamped her legs together. So death is still in the world' (Fleur Adcock).

1977 CRAIG RAINE *Flying to Belfast, 1977* A particularly apt subject for the leader of the Martian school. Surprisingly, given how much flight caught mankind's imagination when it was only a dream, flying has attracted less attraction from poets than might have been thought (though *The Poetry of Flight*, ed. Stella Wolfe, 1925, is a fine compendium of the Biggles school of versification: 'Droning along with rhythmical song / O'er a sandy main in our aeroplane...', etc.)

1978 JAMES FENTON *In a Notebook* Following Auden's example of deliberately courting the danger of a war zone, Fenton went to Vietnam and subsequently Cambodia in 1973 because that 'was just the time the Americans were withdrawing, and so it was obviously going to be a crucial period to see whether the regimes they left behind – the Lon Nol regime in Phnom Penh and the Thiew regime in Saigon – were going to last ... There was obviously going to be a great deal of change. I wanted to see that. I wanted to see a war, and what it was like.' He was one of the few Western journalists to stay in Saigon after its fall, and actually entered the abandoned US Embassy on the turret of a Vietcong tank.

Fenton wrote of himself in 1973, 'I admired the Vietcong and, by extension, the Khmer Rouge...'; 'In a Notebook' is a movingly frank reappraisal of his earlier idealism.

1979　CHRISTOPHER REID　*The Old Soap Opera* A wry requiem for a lost idyll in which, through trade, marriage or the colonial service, the middle classes could treat the world as their oyster.

1980　TOM PAULIN　*Line on the Grass* Paulin has excelled at conveying the drab conditions of life in Northern Ireland during the latest phase of the Troubles.

1981　R. L. CRAWFORD　*Turned Out Nice Again* (from 'The Scrap Heap') In the same summer as the Royal Wedding between Prince Charles and Lady Diana Spencer, seething discontent broke out in rioting and arson in Brixton (April) and Toxteth, Liverpool and Moss Side, Manchester (July). The former was hailed as 'Di Great Insohreckshan' by Linton Kwesi Johnson, while R. L. Crawford's scouse parody of 'The Waste Land' articulated the sense of despair in the economic ghetto of Merseyside. This is the fifth and final section of 'The Scrap Heap'.
　　'Roger Hunt': Liverpool F.C. and England striker.

1982　GAVIN EWART　*England at Christmas, 1982* One of Ewart's many forthright attacks on Mrs Thatcher's regime.
　　'Limited wars': The Falklands.

1983　JOHN WHITWORTH　*These Boys* As though to confirm the Prime Minister's famous declaration 'There's no such thing as society', Britain's social fabric seemed to be disintegrating. Crime figures rose and anxiety about the risk of violence soared. The shocking thing about the incident in 'These Boys' is that it was simply another small crime story reported on local radio.
　　'O bury them deep ... My face is not these faces': synthetic 'Shakespearean' quote intended both to suggest a possible response to the unspeakable, and to highlight the fact that there simply isn't one.

1984　IAN MCMILLAN　*Visitors: Armthorpe, August 1984* Having gained re-election (1983), largely on the strength of the Falklands gamble, Mrs Thatcher turned on 'the enemy within', banning trade union membership at GCHQ Cheltenham and gladly embracing confrontation with the miners, whose strike over proposed pit-closures generated excessive levels of violence.

1985　PETER READING　'*This is unclean*' Reading quickly established himself as the blackest of satirists, and seized on the cruelty and stupidity of fundamentalist bigotry as a natural target, even before the Ayatollah's Fatwa on Salman Rushdie.

1986　WENDY COPE　*My Lover* Wendy Cope combines her talents as parodist (here, of Christopher Smart's 'For I will consider my cat Jeoffrey' from *Jubilato Agno*) and analyst of the pleasures and torments of passion in a love poem which gives perhaps as much contemporary detail as any in the genre.

1987　THOM GUNN　*The Missing* The Aids virus was identified in 1981 in California, and gave rise to the notion of a gay plague. Gunn, who moved to San Francisco in the Fifties, lived through the plague years and published an elegiac collection, *The Man with Night Sweats*, in 1992.

1988 SIMON ARMITAGE *Bus Talk* A distinctive new voice emerging at the end of the Eighties, Armitage exploits a brilliant ear for the demotic to explore areas of life largely neglected previously.

'if you have to pull me out of the rubble ... and half the world there watching': a reference to the televised removal of Norman Tebbit from the ruins of the Grand Hotel, Brighton, after the IRA bomb at the Conservative Party Conference, October 1984.

1989 CAROL ANN DUFFY *Translating the English, 1989* A reflection on the benefits of ten years of Thatcherism.

1990 JACKIE KAY *Death to Poll Tax* The imposition of the hated Poll Tax first in Scotland, then in England and Wales, provoked widespread dissent and many sporadic outbreaks of looting and disorder. It was an error of political judgement that almost certainly contributed to Mrs Thatcher's fall from office: she resigned in November, and was succeeded by John Major.

1991 TONY HARRISON *Initial Illumination* It was the modest and non-triumphalist Major, therefore, who took the country into the Gulf war alongside the Americans and other allies in January 1991 in response to Saddam Hussein's invasion of Kuwait the previous August. Iraq's unbridled aggression and the horrifying vengeance wreaked by the Allies' greatly superior weapons systems posed serious dilemmas for the liberal conscience, which Harrison captures perfectly.

1992 GLYN MAXWELL *Video Tale of a Patriot* Some brands of patriotism have remained virtually unaffected by the passage of time or the unfolding of events.

1993 DON PATERSON *The Scale of Intensity* Helpless armchair viewing of other people's tragedies has been a feature of the Nineties. The break-up of Yugoslavia and the upsurge of militant Serbian nationalism produced massacres and atrocities in Bosnia – the first major blood-letting on the continent since the end of the Second World War.

994 PHILIP GROSS *Postsoviet Postmodern* (from 'A Liminal State' (Estonia, September 1994)) With Communism's tide of faith receding with unforecast rapidity, countries once locked behind the Iron Curtain were left high and dry – free, but in very poor shape. Gross, whose father was an Estonian refugee, went in search of his roots.

1995 ALAN JENKINS *Neighbours* Evidence of the 1994 genocide in which thousands of Tutsi were massacred by Hutu death squads was still coming to light a year later.

1996 JOHN AGARD *Millennium Bug* One aspect of the gathering momentum of the Millennium. Another was the controversial Dome, which the incoming Labour government pledged to continue with.

1997 ANDREW MOTION *Mythology* Princess Diana's death in a car crash in a Paris underpass unleashed an extraordinary outburst of public mourning in Britain and around the world. This elegy appeared on the front page of *The Times* on the day of the funeral, Saturday, 6 September, 1997.

1998 U. A. FANTHORPE *Mother Scrubbing the Floor* A potted social history of the undoubted progress ordinary women have made through the course of the century.

1999 JOHN HEATH-STUBBS *Poem for the End of the World* An engagingly irreverent encapsulation of the various strands of an inevitable apocalyptic foreboding as the end of the century arrives.

'Götterdämmerung': Twilight of the Gods.

ACKNOWLEDGEMENTS

For permission to use copyright material grateful acknowledgement is
made to the following:

DANNIE ABSE: 'After the Release of Ezra Pound' from *Collected Poems
1948–1976* (Hutchinson), by permission of the Peters Fraser & Dunlop
Group Ltd. FLEUR ADCOCK: 'The Soho Hospital for Women' from *Selected
Poems* (Oxford University Press, 1983). JOHN AGARD: 'Millennium Bug'
from *The Devil's Pulpit* (Bloodaxe Books, 1997), by permission of the
publisher. SIMON ARMITAGE: 'Bus Talk' from *Zoom!* (Bloodaxe Books,
1989), by permission of the publisher. W. H. AUDEN: 'A Bride in the 30's'
from *The English Auden: Poems, Essays and Dramatic Writings, 1927–39*,
edited by Edward Mendelson (Faber & Faber, 1986), by permission of the
publisher. HILAIRE BELLOC: 'Ballade of Genuine Concern' from *Complete
Verse* (Pimlico, 1991), by permission of the Peters Fraser & Dunlop Group
Ltd. JAMES BERRY: 'On an Afternoon Train from Purley to Victoria, 1955'
from *News For Babylon* (Chatto & Windus, 1984), by permission of the
author. JOHN BETJEMAN: 'The Town Clerk's Views' from *Collected Poems*
(John Murray, 1958), by permission of the publisher. EDMUND BLUNDEN:
'A Window in Germany August 1939' from *Poems 1930–1940* (Macmillan),
by permission of the Peters Fraser & Dunlop Group Ltd. EDWIN BROCK:
'Five Ways to Kill a Man' from *Five Ways to Kill a Man: New and Selected
Poems* (Enitharmon Press, 1990), by permission of the publisher. BASIL
BUNTING: 'Aus Dem Zweiten Reich' from *The Complete Poems of Basil
Bunting*, edited by Richard Caddel (Oxford University Press, 1994).
CHARLES CAUSLEY: 'Innocent's Song' from *Collected Poems, 1951–1997*
(Macmillan, 1997), by permission of David Higham Associates. G. K.
CHESTERTON: 'A Song of Swords' from *Collected Poems* (Methuen, 1933), by
permission of A. P. Watt Ltd on behalf of The Royal Literary Fund. WENDY
COPE: 'My Lover' from *Making Cocoa for Kingsley Amis* (Faber & Faber,
1997), by permission of the publisher. FRANCES CORNFORD: 'Autumn
Morning at Cambridge' from *Selected Poems* (Enitharmon Press, 1996).
JOHN CORNFORD: 'A Letter from Aragon' from *Understand the Weapon,
Understand the Wound: Selected Writings* (Carcanet Press, 1976), by
permission of the publisher. R. L. CRAWFORD: 'Turned Out Nice Again'
from *The Scrap Heap* (Other Publications, 1982). IDRIS DAVIES: 'Do You
Remember 1926?' from *Gwalia Deserta* (Dent, 1938). W. H. DAVIES: 'A
Beggar's Life' from *Selected Poems* (Oxford University Press, 1985). WALTER
DE LA MARE: 'The Massacre' from *Collected Poems* (Faber & Faber, 1979),
by permission of the Literary Trustees of Walter de la Mare, and The
Society of Authors as their representative. KEITH DOUGLAS: 'Sportsmen'
from *The Complete Poems*, edited by Desmond Graham (Oxford University
Press, 1978). CAROL ANN DUFFY: 'Translating the English, 1989' from *The
Other Country* (Anvil Press Poetry, 1990), by permission of the publisher.
DOUGLAS DUNN: 'Under the Stone' from *The Happier Life* (Faber & Faber,
1972), by permission of the publisher. T. S. ELIOT: 'The Hollow Men' from
Collected Poems, 1909–1962 (Faber & Faber, 1974), by permission of the
publisher. KATHLEEN EMERSON: 'Oh! who are these in scant array ...'

from *Holloway Jingles* (1912). WILLIAM EMPSON: 'Missing Dates' from *Collected Poems* (Chatto & Windus, 1955). D. J. ENRIGHT: 'Changing the Subject' from *Collected Poems, 1948–1998* (Oxford University Press, 1998), by permission of Watson, Little Ltd. GAVIN EWART: 'England at Christmas, 1982' from *The Complete Little Ones* (Hutchinson), by permission of Margo Ewart. U. A. FANTHORPE: 'Mother Scrubbing the Floor' from *Atlantic Review*, Vol. IV, No. 2 (Spring/Summer, 1998), by permission of the author. JAMES FENTON: 'In a Notebook' from *The Memory of War: Poems, 1968–1983* (Penguin International Poets, 1992), by permission of the Peters Fraser & Dunlop Group Ltd. ROY FULLER: 'Pleasure Drive' from *Collected Poems, 1936–1961* (André Deutsch, 1962), by permission of John Fuller. ROBIN FULTON: 'Music of the Spheres' from *The Space Between The Stones Is Where The Survivors Live* (New Rivers Press, 1971). ZULFIKAR GHOSE: 'The Body's Independence' from *Selected Poems* (Karachi: Oxford University Press, 1991), by permission of the publisher. ROBERT GRAVES: 'Song: Lift Boy' from *Complete Poems: Volume 2*, edited by B. Graves and D. Ward (Carcanet Press, 1995), by permission of the publisher. PHILIP GROSS: 'Postsoviet Postmodern' from *The Wasting Game* (Bloodaxe Books, 1998), by permission of the publisher. THOM GUNN: 'The Missing' from *The Man with Night Sweats* (Faber & Faber, 1992), by permission of the publisher. IVOR GURNEY: 'Daily - Old Tale' from *Collected Poems of Ivor Gurney*, edited by P. J. Kavanagh (Oxford University Press, 1982). TONY HARRISON: 'Initial Illumination' from *A Cold Coming: Gulf War Poems* (Bloodaxe Books, 1991), by permission of the author. JOHN HEATH-STUBBS: 'Poem for the End of the World' from *Agenda*, Volume 35, No. 4 (1997). A. P. HERBERT: 'The General Inspecting the Trenches' from *The Somme* by Lyn Macdonald (Penguin Books, 1993), by permission of A. P. Watt Ltd on behalf of Crystal Hale and Jocelyn Hale. GEOFFREY HILL: 'The Guardians' from *For the Unfallen* (André Deutsch, 1971). GEOFFREY HOLLOWAY: 'Rhine Jump, 1944' from *Rhine Jump* (London Magazine Editions, 1974), by permission of Alan Ross. A. E. HOUSMAN: 'Eight o'Clock' from *Last Poems* (Grant Richards, 1922), by permission of The Society of Authors as the literary representative of the Estate of A. E. Housman. ELIZABETH JENNINGS: 'The Planners' from *Collected Poems* (Carcanet Press, 1986), by permission of David Higham Associates. TED HUGHES: 'A Disaster' from *Crow: From the Life and Songs of the Crow* (Faber & Faber, 1995). ALAN JENKINS: 'Neighbours' from *The Times Literary Supplement*. JACKIE KAY: 'Death to Poll Tax' from *The Adoption Papers* (Bloodaxe Books, 1991), by permission of the publisher. RUDYARD KIPLING: 'The Sons of Martha' from *Selected Poems* (Penguin Twentieth Century Classics, 1993), by permission of A. P. Watt Ltd on behalf of The National Trust for Places of Historic Interest or Natural Beauty. PHILIP LARKIN: 'High Windows' from *Collected Poems*, edited by Anthony Thwaite (Faber & Faber, 1988), by permission of the publisher. D. H. LAWRENCE: 'Change of Government' from *The Complete Poems of D. H. Lawrence* (Penguin Twentieth Century Classics, 1994), by permission of Laurence Pollinger Ltd and the Estate of Frieda Lawrence Ravagli. MICHAEL LONGLEY: 'Wounds' from *Poems, 1963–1983* (Secker & Warburg, 1991). HUGH MACDIARMID: 'After Two Thousand Years' from *Complete Poems: 2 Volumes*, edited by M. Grieve and W. R. Aitken (Carcanet Press. 1993, 1994), by permission of the publisher. LOUIS MACNEICE: from 'Autumn Journal' from *Collected Poems* (Faber & Faber, 1979), by permission of David Higham Associates. ROGER MCGOUGH: 'Let

Me Die a Youngman's Death' from *The Mersey Sound: Penguin Modern Poets 10*, with Adrian Henri and Brian Patten (Penguin Books, 1967), by permission of the Peters Fraser & Dunlop Group Ltd on behalf of the author. IAN MCMILLAN: 'Visitors: Armthorpe, August 1984' from *Selected Poems* (Carcanet Press, 1987). JOHN MASEFIELD: 'Cargoes' from *Selected Poems* (Heinemann, 1978), by permission of The Society of Authors as the literary representative of the Estate of John Masefield. GLYN MAXWELL: 'Video Tale of a Partriot' from *Out of the Rain* (Bloodaxe Books, 1992), by permission of the publisher. G. K. MENZIES: 'Frames of Mind' from *Punch* (22 June 1904). ADRIAN MITCHELL: 'Order Me a Transparent Coffin' from *Heart on the Left: Poems 1953–1984* (Bloodaxe Books, 1997), by permission of the Peters Fraser & Dunlop Group Ltd on behalf of the author. *Educational Health Warning!* Adrian Mitchell asks that none of his poems are used in connection with any examinations whatsoever. NAOMI MITCHISON: 'The Midsummer Apple Tree' from *Time and Tide* (1 July 1933), by permission of David Higham Associates Ltd. EDWIN MORGAN: 'From Cathkin Braes: a View of Korea' from *Collected Poems* (Carcanet Press, 1990), by permission of the publisher. ANDREW MOTION: 'Mythology' from *The Times* (6 September 1997), by permission of the Peters Fraser & Dunlop Group Ltd. EDWIN MUIR: 'The Interrogation' from *Collected Poems* (Faber & Faber, 1984), by permission of the publisher. PAUL MULDOON: 'Dancers at the Moy' from *New Weather* (Faber & Faber, 1973), by permission of the publisher. HAROLD MUNRO: 'Midnight Lamentation' from *Collected Poems* (Cobden-Sanderson, 1933). DON PATERSON: 'The Scale of Intensity' from *God's Gift to Women* (Faber & Faber, 1997), by permission of the publisher. TOM PAULIN: 'Line on the Grass' from *The Strange Museum* (Faber & Faber, 1980), by permission of the publisher. SYLVIA PLATH: 'Lady Lazarus' from *Collected Poems* (Faber & Faber, 1981), by permission of the publisher. PETER PORTER: 'At the Castle Hotel, Taunton' from *Collected Poems* (Oxford University Press, 1999). EZRA POUND: from 'Hugh Selwyn Mauberley' from *Collected Shorter Poems* (Faber & Faber, 1984), by permission of the publisher. CRAIG RAINE: 'Flying to Belfast, 1977' from *The Onion Memory* (Oxford University Press, 1978). PETER READING: 'This is unclean ...' from *Collected Poems: 2: Poems 1985–1996* (Bloodaxe Books, 1996), by permission of the author and publisher. HENRY REED: 'Naming of Parts' from *A Map of Verona* (Jonathan Cape, 1947). CHRISTOPHER REID: 'The Old Soap Opera' from *Arcadia* (Oxford University Press, 1979). EDGELL RICKWORD: 'Luxury' from *Collected Poems* (Carcanet Press, 1991). ANNE RIDLER: 'Choosing a Name' from *New & Selected Poems* (Faber & Faber, 1988). ALAN ROSS: ''Survivors', by permission of the author. SIEGFRIED SASSOON: 'The Effect' from *The War Poems* (Faber & Faber, 1983), copyright Siegfried Sassoon, by kind permission of George Sassoon. DAVID SCOTT: 'Winston Churchill' from *Selected Poems* (Bloodaxe Books, 1998), by permission of the publisher. JON SILKIN: 'Death of a Son' from *Selected Poems* (Routledge, 1988). STEVIE SMITH: 'Touch and Go' from *The Collected Poems of Stevie Smith* (Penguin Twentieth Century Classics, 1989), by permission of James MacGibbon. STEPHEN SPENDER: 'The Express' from *Collected Poems, 1928–85* (Faber & Faber, 1985), by permission of the publisher. DYLAN THOMAS: 'Among Those Killed ...' from *Collected Poems* (Dent, 1971), by permission of David Higham Associates. R. S. THOMAS: 'The Village' from *Poems, 1946–68* (Bloodaxe Books, 1992). PHILLIP WHITFIELD: 'Day of Liberation, Bergen-Belsen, May 1945' from *The Voice of War: Poems of the Second World War*, edited by Victor Selwyn (Michael Joseph, 1995), by permission of The Salamander Oasis Trust. JOHN WHITWORTH: 'These Boys' from *Lovely Day For A Wedding* (Secker & Warburg, 1985), by permission of the author. ANNA WICKHAM: 'Divorce' from *The Writings of Anna Wickham: Free Woman and Poet*, edited by R. D. Smith (Virago, 1984), by permission of George Hepburn and Margaret Hepburn. W. B. YEATS: 'The Second Coming' from *Collected Poems* (Picador, 1990), by permission of A. P. Watt Ltd on behalf of Michael B. Yeats.

Every effort has been made to trace or contact all copyright holders. The publishers would be pleased to rectify any omissions brought to their notice at the earliest opportunity.